You Can INVADE THE IMPOSSIBLE through Prayer

Can you learn to pray with power and effect? The answer is a resounding "yes!" according to author Jack Hayford, pastor of a California church that is gaining nationwide attention through its emphasis on prayer as a dynamic possibility for every member.

Do you yearn to pray effectively, but don't know how even to begin? Then this book is for you.

To Jack Hayford, prayer is not the mystical experience of a few special people, but an aggressive act in the face of impossibility—an act that may be performed by anyone who will accept the challenge to learn to pray.

Here is a practical "how-to" book that will get you started on the road to effective prayer.

Prayer is
INVADING
THE
IMPOSSIBLE

JACK W. HAYFORD

Prayer is
INVADING
THE
IMPOSSIBLE

JACK W. HAYFORD

Logos International
Plainfield, New Jersey

PRAYER IS INVADING THE IMPOSSIBLE
Copyright © 1977 by Logos International
All rights reserved
Printed in the United States of America
International Standard Book Number: 0-88270-218-1
Library of Congress Catalog Card Number: 77-71684
Published by Logos International, Plainfield, New Jersey 07061

INTRODUCTION

"Receive . . . knowledge rather than choice gold." Proverbs *8:10*

"Now, wait just a minute. I'm a born-again Christian with eternity taken care of and my spiritual experience is bronzed and hanging on the rear-view mirror of my '57 Chevy and don't tell me anything that makes me feel uncomfortable because I don't need anymore stretch-marks!"

Usually, when I make a statement like that, it's because the Holy Spirit has just spoken through our pastor, Jack Hayford, and there's a need to let the fresh understanding set larger boundaries for God's rulership in my heart. The Lord Jesus is calling believers to a deeper understanding of our function on this planet and many of us are afraid of that call because additional spiritual growth just might mean getting stuck with additional spiritual responsibility. Or, worse yet, we might get trapped into a pattern of unending enlargement! Heaven forbid!

Or, does heaven prescribe it?

Jack Hayford feels it does. The services at "The Church on the Way" are filled with the sweet presence of the Spirit of God, alongside challenges from the Word to live a richer, deeper, more fruitful life in Jesus. What's being taught from up front is not "dead religiosity" but how the living truth can be so rooted in human lives that people become extenders of God's purpose wherever they walk.

In 1970, Pastor Hayford was at prayer in his parent's living room in northern California, when the Holy Spirit showed him, in his mind's eye, a picture of what appeared to be a trophy. It was the kind of prize that might be awarded to an athlete for winning a race. Written on tne trophy was the word "Position."

The Lord spoke to his heart and said, "Will you give it back to me?"

Jack had always been a leader and felt that his leadership ability was a gift from God. He had never considered giving back what came from the creator's own hand. His mind was flooded with memories of events in which he had been in a leadership position.

"Will you give it back to me?"

The knowledge came that God would love him just as much if he did not give up "Position"; but he was revulsed by the sudden discovery of how important it was for him to be "the leader."

Although it was his long-held desire to pastor a large congregation, he did not seem to be making much progress in drumming up a crowd. He had pastored the church in Van Nuys for nine months and there were still only sixty-five people in attendance.

Could be give up all hope of ever leading a large church? He realized, with dismay, that he had been holding himself above his small pastorate.

"Yes, Lord, I give it back to you. Yes, Lord Jesus, I surrender position, and ambition, and leadership into your hands."

He rose from his knees filled with a perfect peace, even though he fully believed that he would live out his life as the pastor of a small church.

He returned to Los Angeles and the following Sunday night, the congregation *doubled* in number!

"Good grief," he thought, "the place is packed!" He could not resist counting heads. There was no way to escape the fact that while Jack Hayford was away, the Lord was building His Church.

In Jack's wildest dreams, he could not have imagined that

such growth would continue and that six years later a typical Sunday would see four thousand turned-on sons and daughters of the eternal Father worshiping where that tiny "packed house" assembled. Possibly because the emphasis has never shifted to numbers, God still adds new lives each week.

My wife, Lory, and I, at the suggestion of a Jewish friend, visited the Church on the Way one day in 1974. We sensed the reality of the presence of God in the hearts of those gathered there, and coming back to the evening service, we publicly confessed Jesus Christ as the Lord of our lives.

A miracle happened in our spirits! A miracle that could not have grown nor borne fruit without the teaching ministry of a shepherd who is open to what the Holy Spirit of God would say through him.

"Invading the Impossible" shares with all of us what Pastor Hayford is being taught about prayer. The words pour forth, creating an atomosphere thick with the knowledge of God. Don't be afraid of the depths into which you're being called.

Four years ago, the church was led into intercessory prayer for the nation. We were not the only group praying for the healing of our land, but we were to pray as if we were.

In this last election, we had a choice of several professing believers . . . an answer to prayer that righteous men be raised to high political office.

We prayed that God would raise up many intercessors . . . and then financed a touring company of the musical production "If My People . . ." (II Chronicles 7:14) to sixty cities . . . 150,000 believers committed themselves to intercessory prayer.

God answers believing prayer! Just recently, the church sang requests to the Father on behalf of a ten-year-old girl who was about to have her legs amputated. Each person in the congregation sang a prayer of his own making, asking God to restore those little legs. God did. We did not find out until later that the child was a ballet dancer.

This book may change forever some of your ideas about praying. Allow the Holy Spirit to move you with the reality of the truth and then fearlessly let Jesus minister through you to a small child or to a whole nation.

Dean Jones
February 1977

CONTENTS

Prayer is
INVADING
THE
IMPOSSIBLE

JACK W. HAYFORD

PART ONE

One world speaks:
> *To hope when there is no hope is*
> *the mark of a fool.*

Another world answers:
> *The foolishness of God*
> *is wiser than men.*

1.
INVADING THE IMPOSSIBLE

Her eyes were flooded with fear and shame. Society had adopted the word "gay" to define her condition, but nothing could be further from the lightheartedness the word used to describe. Her plea: "Is there a way out for me? I'm so afraid . . . and so very, very tired."

His voice was taut. Her hands were wringing. "She's been gone for days now," he said of his daughter. "We know where she is, but we don't know what to do. It's such a mess. We've tried to figure out where we may be responsible, but even our best efforts at love don't seem to dent her. We're up against a wall."

His eyes flitted to avoid direct gaze with mine: "Jack, I don't know how to say it, . . . I uh. . . ." His uncertainty sputtered on his lips. The problem: he was involved with another woman. His wife, whom he truly loved, was entirely unaware of it. His difficulty was not his need to be convinced of his failing, but to find a way to break the controlling grip he felt on his soul, which repeatedly dragged him into compromise and infidelity.

People addicted. Or bound by destructive habits.

Businesses shipwrecked on rocks of economic reversals.

Marriages with the love wrung out of them—and society asserting that divorce is the answer.

Medical reports silently screaming, "Cancer!"

Children exploding into unpredictable behavior patterns.

Bills towering above an overdrawn checkbook.

Jobs disappearing and unemployment offering a way to nowhere.

Long-term hopes dissolved.

Constant pain from a physical problem that knows no reprieve.

Recurring frustration with a personal deficiency that can't be overcome.

Blockades on the highway to happiness.

Bulletin boards affixed with blank papers.

Wondering what to do next.

Having tried anything and everyone.

Futility.

Face-to-face with impossibility—or what seems like it.

Everybody comes here at some time. Some more frequently than others. Positive thinking disappears as a useable tool, except perhaps for the more intensely tenacious personality. Faith dims for all except the most rock-like saint. And at this point you're ready for an answer.

Ready, because you're desperate.

Ready, because you've tried everything else.

Ready, because your attention has been gained.

Ready, because there's actually nothing else you can do. At this point you're ready to pray.

Pray?

Ready to pray?

As an escape from reality?
As a flight into some kind of guesswork?
As an emotional release that doesn't change anything?
As a blind shot at hope with no idea where the target is?
No.
But ready to pray truly.
　To pray as an entrance into reality.
　To pray as a trip with predestined certainty.
　To pray as an experience of intelligently based peace.
　To pray with the knowledge you are on target every time.

The impossible faces us all.
　It storms, fumes,
　　looms before us,
　　　stalks our days,
　　　　presses upon our minds,
bends our plans,
　stands formidably across our future,
　　pierces our present,
　　　reaches out from our past.

But there is a way to face impossibility.
　Invade it!
　　Not with a glib speech of high hopes.
　　　Not in anger.
　　Not with resignation.
　　　Not through stoical self-control.
But with violence.
And prayer provides the vehicle for this kind of violence.

Everyone acknowledges the expertise of the trained professional until we come to theology. Then, everyone's an expert.

2.
ANYONE CAN DO IT,
CAN'T THEY?

Take your pick, because they all have a bad press. Society doesn't leap with expectancy over any of these words:
God.
Church.
Bible.
Jesus.
Prayer.
Most guess about the first,
get disgusted with the second,
   can't understand the third,
      use the fourth to swear,
And then . . .
   however ineffectively or imperfectly,
we all try the last one.

Sometime or another, everyone prays.
The emotional person may weep, the bewildered may mutter to themselves, the sophisticate may not admit it, the

9

intellectual may say he "just expressed an inner affirmation."
But they all prayed.

That acknowledgment is not, however, to suggest they did it well. But marvelously, for reasons that ought to and can be understood, prayer—fumbling, halting, fearful, dubious, well-worded, whispered or unspokenly wished—works.

In fact, it works so well by apparent accident it's puzzling that more don't bother to find out how it works in actuality. It works so well in a crisis, one wonders why we don't implement it on a regular basis.

Most of us don't pray on a regular basis because we're deeply aware that it will cost us something.

More than time.

More than money.

More than faith.

More than becoming religious.

To lay hold of prayer as my own available resource for effective, practical, daily use—as an abiding certainty in an unpredictable world—will cost me one thing.

Honesty.

I may grasp at prayer in an emergency;

    lunge for some divine intervention in the face of my helplessness;

        call to God in the middle of my painful difficulty;

        and make a connection.

    Thank God! It worked!!

    Why?

Because my obvious need forced my hand. I had to tell Him—somebody "up there," God, the "Man Upstairs," whoever *you* are—that I couldn't handle it myself.

That's what really started the action. My honest confession of impotence opened the door to omnipotence. That's how "sometime" answers are secured.

But we're after constant answers: certainty in the midst of uncertainty; possibilities where there seem to be none remaining. But such prayer will require more than just honesty about our helplessness.

That's a beginning.

But it will also require real honesty about our ignorance.

Sin—that old-fashioned word about humanity that asserts that none of us really have it completely together—is a two-headed monstrous reality in us all. It labels our inadequacy for continued unselfish goodness, and it describes our mental blindness to the truths that make prayer not only a viable, but a vital way of life.

Honesty requires acknowledgment of what we aren't. And there's nothing more inherent in human nature than the insistency that we can do it ourselves, and "I'm going to do it my way, too!"

So, we don't pray.

At least not until we can't do it ourselves. Not until our way didn't work . . . nor did any of the dozen other ways we tried. (And even then there are those who will "be damned" if they'll play the hypocrite and call on God in a crisis. Their inverted honesty argues, "I didn't believe in a God when things were all right, so I'm not going to cop out now with some childish flight into fantasy.")

Honesty refusing its own exercise. How ironic.

But abstract honesty isn't the price of prayer. Not just "honest-to-myself" honesty.

No.

Only "honest-to-God" honesty will do it.

Honesty which acknowledges our obvious need for forgiveness and inner fullness;

Honesty which admits the draining effect our own compromising has had on us, and

Honesty which refuses to compromise further with another

11

artificial answer for our emptiness.

Such honesty will receive the record of history regarding the only one who ever claimed to be the giver of real fullness in life and to be the sole way to God. It will confront a history which records His miraculous birth, impeccable life, phenomenal teaching, dynamic miracles, atoning death, and glorious resurrection.

His history may not be undeniable, but it is irrefutable. Anyone can shut out the sunshine, but no one can stop the dawn.

Or high noon!

After we initially open to His life and power, we will need to learn what He really came for. If we think that the "hope of heaven" is the sum of Christ's gift, we will live out a spiritually juvenile existence, pointed toward heaven but pointless on earth.

Perhaps the high point of Jesus' teaching ministry came when His disciples asked Him, "Lord, teach us to pray." When pupils ask the right questions, the teacher is happiest.

In response, Jesus taught them nothing of mysticism, nothing of religious pretense, nothing of meditation, nothing of bizarre physical contortions, nor anything of memorized incantations attended by clouds of incense.

But He did teach them something about a matter of violence.

He was very clear on that one thing.

Prayer was a matter of assault,
   of binding,
   of warfare,
   of invasion.

On earthside, He taught, things may appear impossible, yet, from the heavenside of things, there is a violence that can explode the impossible.

But it needs troops for the invasion.

About two feet ahead
and slightly to the left, son,
there's an entry point
into a better realm than ours.
The problem is finding how to catch up with it!

3.
A WORLD WAITING
IN THE WINGS

To understand prayer we need to realize what Jesus came to do. That's because our prayer will express God's purpose as Christ revealed it. And His purpose is *repossession.*

That's the word.

To summarize the whole of the Bible in eight statements:

1. God created man to enjoy earth and inhabit it as a king does his domain, unhindered by any power that would diminish the quality of life God had given.

2. Man's rule of earth—God-given and God-ordained—was lost through disobedience. The control of the planet was forfeited to Satan, whose goal is to deprive man of God's intended purpose and destroy all hope of recovery.

3. God established Israel to teach man His desire for man's recovered rulership. By renewed obedience to God joyous and peaceful living may be realized—personally and nationally.

4. Against a backdrop of man's failure to learn this lesson, God entered the human scene. "The Word became flesh." The life, which was the light of man, shone into the darkness. The Word spoke.

15

5. He spoke consistently of a kingdom. "The kingdom of God is immediately at hand," Jesus proclaimed. He spoke authoritatively of the fact that the earth's original ruler—God—was available. If man would receive his king, he could enjoy a renewed dominion of peace and joy here and now.

6. For His claim to be God's Messiah, here to restore God's rule, He was crucified. But by a power unknown to man, the blood of the cross became the means of breaking Satan's hold on the power of death. Jesus rose again and commissioned His forces (He called them "a church") to bring His world of God's restoring rulership to bear upon the world of Satan's destroying rulership.

7. The ultimate message of the Bible is that Christ will return to drive out the last vestiges of Satan's operations on earth.

But,

8. In the meantime, His church has been commissioned to walk the pathway to restored rulership. Jesus has committed the "keys of the kingdom" to those who know and obey Him. These keys are fitted to:

a. Stop hell's worst and insist on heaven's best.

b. Unlock mankind's captives and shatter Satan's chains.

Almost everyone knows that the Lord Jesus Christ promised to return again. But too few of us realize that in the interim we are not merely charged to witness of His love while waiting for His return. We are also explicitly commanded to introduce His rulership—the kingdom of God—into those circumstances in which man's lost rule has produced impossible situations.

Christ's whole life presents a clear picture of two kingdoms in opposition. That picture may be seen in instances where—

Truth confronts the universal Liar,

Reality exposes the sham of Religiosity,

Health crashes into the domain of Sickness,

Deliverance unshackles spiritual Bondage,
Love overflows the depths of Human Fear,
Forgiveness expels the condemnation Guilt produces,
Wholeness expands the constriction Sin works.

The substance of His teaching is given force by the triumph
of His cross. In becoming the ultimate casualty of sin—God
dying for man—He exhausted the dynamic of death in
whatever form it may take:
Death of soul, which sin works;
Death of hope, which despair brings;
Death of love, which strife produces;
Death of understanding, which bigotry accomplishes;
Death of comfort, with which pain torments us;
Death of body, which is humankind's final blow.

Those operations of the kingdom of hell took the life of the
king of all. If there were ever an ultimate impossibility, it was
in a sealed tomb in Jerusalem twenty centuries ago. Every
casualty of life's frustrations, dilemmas, weaknesses,
temptations, sinnings, sicknesses, pains, sorrows, heartaches
and hopelessness is to be served notice: *He happened for you!*

The ultimate casualty has swallowed up all other
hell-workings in himself and, triumphing over them in His
cross, has risen from the dead! The inability of hell's prince to
contain heaven's king unfolds the practical implications of
Jesus'message transmitted to us:

There's a world waiting in the wings.

The world you live in is not irretrievably trapped by its own
limitations. Since I have triumphed over death, you may learn
to rule in life.

17

Rulership in life is the option Christ offers. Rule—dominion—victory—triumph—conquest. But no experience of rulership is without contest. The adversary still contends for earth-rule, and until Christ finally expels all his workings, his conquest is experienced only through warfare. Each believer is a member of an occupational force which has one principal purpose: *to enforce the victory of Calvary.*

It is in this context that prayer begins to take shape. It becomes more than a single-dimensioned "asking." It becomes a multifaceted weapon through supplication, intercession, praise, thanksgiving, travail, petition and worship. Each of these means of prayer is expedited by the understanding believer's employment of the many means to prayer, like agreeing, praying with the understanding, singing, praying with the spirit, laying on of hands and bearing one another's burdens.

"Praying with all prayer" is the final exhortation of the greatest single passage in the Bible on the subject of spiritual warfare. Clearly, then, the order which Jesus introduced with His message of "a kingdom," and for which He wrestled unto death to secure as an abiding availability to mankind, is waiting to enter wherever His ambassadors will declare it.

No bastion will fall without a battle, but no battle will be lost if the warfare is fought according to the captain's commands:

"Watch and pray."

"This kind comes out only by prayer and fasting."

"Men ought always to pray and not to faint."

"Pray without ceasing."

"Praying with all prayer . . ." and so the battle goes.

It's an act of violence, prayer is.

Wrenching Satan's claws from God's property, redeemed through the blood of the cross of God's Son—we need to learn well how to go about it.

18

There is a shock wave more unsettling
than an earthquake,
more irresistible
than a tidal wave,
more uncontrollable
than a tornado . . .
but a thousand times more desirable
than any of them.

4.
THE VIOLENCE OF LIFE

Although the full release of this power would not be available to mankind until after Jesus' death and resurrection, He nevertheless threatened the forces of hell as never before from the moment He began to announce His new kingdom.

John the Baptist had proclaimed His coming. What the prophets had foretold, he said, was now on the brink of occurring.

And it did.

When Jesus was baptized in the Jordan, the Holy Spirit came upon Him. This was the day of the king's anointing and from that hour the adversary knew the duration and durability of his kingdom were in question. The open warfare began with the temptation in the wilderness, in which—like a wary wrestler—Satan tried his opponent with two approaches before his open attack with the crucial question. "All right," he said, as it were, "we both know what this is all about. It's man's earth, isn't it? Man's earth which I've taken and rule."

The Son didn't answer.

"You think you'll take it somehow. But consider an

immediate possibility." He paused for effect. "It's yours. The kingdoms of this world . . . all yours. But one requirement."

The serpent's hiss can be heard yet.

"Bow down and worship me, for I am the one who owns title right to mankind and his domain."

The king's rebuke was instant and conclusive.

"Begone, Liar. The Most High . . . He is God, and He alone is worthy of worship."

Jesus' denial of Satan's offer is significant not only in His refusal of the lying option afforded Him, but also in the fact that He does not challenge Satan's claim to the right of rulership over the kingdoms of this world. The stakes were real and entirely in his control. Jesus was the Outsider.

But the Outside was moving Inside.

A planet acclimated to death and dying, to sickness and suffering, to weakness and failure, to sin and strife, to war and heartbreak, to trouble and tragedy, to division and divorce—to accepting the insolubility of the impossible—was being invaded.

The invading force was only one. But that One was the creator of all, who from the beginning had calculated a plan which would not only mystify the enemy and release his prisoners; it would introduce the redeemed to a pathway of sharing with Him in His conquest.

So it began to happen.

Life was beginning to infect the poisoned planet with health. Love was beginning to flow purely into the muddied cisterns of man's being.

But when a planet's inhabitants are accustomed to fear and death and when the liar who rules them has adequately convinced them that these traits and all that goes with them are normal, such an invasion will only stimulate violent resistance which only violence overcomes.

Jesus said of His ministry: "Since its beginning, the kingdom of God is allowing for violence, and the violent are breaking into its possibilities."

Life was entering the area of death. The resultant destruction was not "violent" as we usually think of it. It was violent in that an age-long bondage of mankind to alien domination was being destroyed. When a higher power lays claim to the domain of a lower power, the lesser must yield. When love and life face fear and death, the latter lose.

The Son of God was forcibly—by the authority of His Word, manifested by the power-workings of the Holy Spirit of God—exacting this ageless agreement:

The God of the heavens is above all.

The adversary did not yield agreeably to that power, but his lesser authority had no ground to retain except where unbelieving men would continue to hold the planet in rebellion. Wherever other men submitted to the new king of glory, His dominion entered.

This entry works so great an upheaval in the ordinary course of human experience, the king referred to it as new birth. Birth is violent. It is not without blood, pain, stretching, agony and travail. "The violent are breaking into the kingdom," the king said.

All the while, as His ministry gains momentum and many men burst into life with Him, He is moving toward the master stroke geared to completely outwit the agencies of darkness.

The councils of heaven have conceived the plan before all time, and in its execution—which is discharged upon the Son himself—the wisdom of God is confounding the stratagems of Satan.

In surrendering to the agony, the blood, the pain, the travail and the stretching involved in His suffering on the cross, Jesus gave birth to a new creation—a new world.

All is violence at Calvary, but life is winning the day. Afterward, it is quiet in the garden of burials, while on Golgotha lingering imps chortle with glee. But in hell, the alarm has been sounded. The halls of death are echoing with the trumpeting of a voice unlike any they have heard since the day the Almighty consigned them to the abyss. "It's Him again," they are shrieking. "We thought we had won. We thought we had Him!" But He's announcing their ultimate doom, enunciating each word with authoritative clarity as He reaches unhindered to take the keys of death and hell from the arch-deceiver's gnarled fist. In one swath of life-splendor He is unleashing the righteous dead from their comfortable waiting-place on the peaceful shores of the underworld. They are being transferred this day to the eternal Father's presence, while the wicked remain in Hades' shadowed flame to have their eternal judgment underscored by this drastic alteration in the structure of the spirit world.

It may be helpful to introduce an analogy here from the Second World War. Just as Hitler's doom was assured after the battle of Stalingrad in 1943, although troops did not enter Berlin until 1945, so the ultimate defeat of Satan was secured at Calvary, although much struggle yet awaits the church on its way to the consummation.

The violence which life is working in the midst of death has penetrated to the throne of Satan. The God of the heavens has spoken, hell has been shaken, and earth will never be the same again.

Nothing is more limiting than the self-imposed boundaries we clamp around our own lives when we require God to fit into our expectations.

5.
THE FORCE OF A
REAL EXPERIENCE

The first wave of blessing had emanated from a tomb where a man had been wrapped in death. The second from a room where some men had hid in fear, and now were waiting in prayer.

Pentecost.

Birthday.

A strapping baby church.

And my how it grew!

Jesus, first-born from the dead, had smashed hell's gates and loosed a force that had restructured the spirit world. Now the Holy Spirit is breaking in upon a handful of followers who have proven obedient to Jesus' directive:

Don't attempt your mission to mankind with the message I've given until you have received the dynamic essential to document the truth you speak.

Their waiting was not passive. It was obedient and filled with prayer. "These continued with one accord in prayer and supplication," the record reports. The week between the Ascension and Pentecost was given to one thing—prayer. Like a fetus, bent in the womb awaiting birth, the church was bending in prayer awaiting its destined date of beginning with power.

There is no evidence that those early believers knew for certain either what they were going to experience or when it would take place. All they knew was that their Lord had promised them that something powerful would happen, and if they waited on Him He would see they received it.

Unfortunately, the church's official attitude differs in this regard today. On the subject of "receiving power" as Jesus ordered, each segment of the church is somehow convinced that it knows both exactly what that means and, with virtual precision, when it happens.

Two things are clear about that day of Pentecost: when it happened they understood, and what happened we are told exactly. We would be wise today if we ceased our pneumatological theologizing (creedal dictums on the Holy Spirit) and let believers pray—to wait in prayer upon the person of their Lord. To wait, not in doubt or mindless gropings, but in humble preparation of the heart and in simple worship of the Lord God. The "beauty of holiness" kind of worship doesn't happen with a smear of religious cosmetic applied in a minute's pause before the open compact of some dogmatized idea of "Holy Spirit fullness." Real transformation from phlegmatic uncertainty into confident ministry takes awhile. "With open face we look into the mirror of His Word and become transformed by His presence; this is done by the ministry of the Spirit of the Lord."

If believers will come *in prayer* to Jesus—who alone is accredited as the official baptizer-with-the-Holy-Spirit—they will receive the timeless promise of divine enablement (Acts 2:39). They will not earn this experience with prayer, but they will receive it through prayer. And while faith is the instrument

28

by which all God's provision is reached for, experience is the criterion for judging whether faith has been effective. The church, which was born to shake a world from the adversary's control, knew they had received the promised power. They did not say: "We received by faith," in answer to inquiring onlookers who puzzled over what was transpiring as the wine of heaven was filling the church on earth, but they declared: This Jesus God raised up again, to which we are all witnesses. Therefore having been exalted to the right hand of God, and having received from the Father the promise of the Holy Spirit, He has poured forth this which you both see and hear (Acts 2:32, 33 NAS).

They knew they had received the promise Jesus had told them to await. They had prayed until it happened. That it had they knew, and so did those looking on.

They also were concerned whenever other new believers didn't share in this aspect of believing life. Peter and John's ministry among the newly redeemed in Samaria (Acts 8:15), and Paul's inquiry of the Ephesian believers upon his arrival (Acts 19:1-12) clearly demonstrates a basic posture in the early church. In essence it was: "We're under instructions to change the world. Once you have been rescued from it, you'll need power to become a threat to it. The world which contained you in its grasp until now will not release its hold on others without a fight. Power is the key to our victory, and prayer is the pathway to power."

People who came to know the redeeming love of God in Jesus Christ were taught and led to pray that they might be filled with the Holy Spirit. There doesn't seem to be any theological argumentation or formulated requirements of verification. But people did pray, and when they had made contact with heaven, they did know it.

It is wonderful for the believer to lay aside doctrinal and

dogmatic arguments and formulas, and pray. And if you are seeking some guideline to know if you've been filled with or baptized in the Holy Spirit, it would probably be wisest to seek it from the uncluttered Word of God. Formulas engender fear of not "performing" correctly, dogmas engender brittleness which hinder liberty in the Lord, and virtually all human doctrinal constructions leave something to be desired.

"Draw near unto God, and He will draw near to you."
"Humble yourselves therefore under the mighty hand of God, that He may exalt you in due time."

Prayer opens the doorway to the dynamic that shakes, shatters and does violence to the world of darkness. Hell's forces hold no respect for our attempts to match its wit or its workings.

But it was forced to yield ground to those believers who prayed until they received power.

It still will if we will.

When subnormal is normal,
normalcy is labeled abnormal
and real sense said to make none.

6.
ON MAKING UPSIDE-DOWN
RIGHT-SIDE-UP
AND HAVING IT CALLED
UPSIDE-DOWN

Few things have contributed to spiritual barrenness in the church Christ founded as has the idea that prayer is mere quiet, meditational passivism.

There is a time to be silent. There is a time to be still. To know the awesomeness of God's person and presence.

But prayer is alive.

It is aloud with praise,
    aglow with warmth,
    attuned with song,
    aflame with power.

And it is also unsettling in its violence.

Not in the violence of its practice, but in the violence of its impact when it is exercised with power.

Thessalonica, a city of ancient Greece, was where the first accurate assessment was made of what was going on through the living force of the church Jesus had begun. It wasn't intended as a compliment, but as the foundation of civil charges being leveled against a small contingent of believers: "These

that have turned the world upside down are come hither also"
(Acts 17:6).

The next verse asserts the grounds of their complaint: "They
do contrary to the decrees of Caesar, saying that there is
another king, one Jesus."

There it is.

Kingship . . . kingdom . . . who's in charge, is at the root of
the complaint.

And it's clear there was more than just a teaching being
called into question. Things were happening too. "The world is
being turned upside down."

The progress since Pentecost had not been dramatic in
chronological terms. The tremors which began that day were
strong, to say the least. But their geographical spread from that
epicenter had been gradual. It was eight years before it made
its force felt only thirty miles north in Samaria.

A short time later Antioch, an important city in Syria, was
experiencing such a measure of quaking in its cultural life that
this new breed of people received a coined name: Christians.
The term was a mocking epithet. But the world recognized it
was being challenged by something it hadn't seen before.

Now an additional seven years had gone by and the record of
a growing history about this clan was being circulated across
the face of the Roman Empire. Throughout the provinces of
Asia Minor, city after city had felt the surge of this order of life
entering. But when people are accustomed to death as a life
style, real life becomes a violent option. It's upsetting. Nothing
will mess up cemeteries like resurrections!

"These that have turned the world upside down have come
to us." A world used to its backward, wrong-side-up-ness, was
being confronted by a rectifying power that was reversing the
control of the present order of things. The citizens thought it
was Caesar's power which was being challenged. It wasn't. It

34

was Satan's.

They were right, however, in their recognition that it had to do with the proclamation of a new king. A transfer of rulership between gods doesn't take place by an orderly process. The god of this world was being progressively dethroned on earth by the Son of the God of the heavens. What had happened in the underworld was happening on the surface of things. The violence of the victor was being extended by His troops. They were invading the realm where the liar had sold his citizens on death, and told them "that's life." The abnormal and perverted were being unveiled for what they were, and human philosophizing about relativism and individualism was becoming manifestly impractical. The order of disorder was dissolving, and the entrance of God's order was disconcerting.

When you're used to living upside down, right side up seems wrong.

We need to notice two things:

1. The havoc being worked by heaven was beneficial to earth-man and only destructive to hell-power.

2. The power which brought this healing, life and freedom to individuals had a basic pattern to its spread: a combination of pure power working holy havoc.

To illustrate this idea, let us examine the Book of the Acts of the Apostles.

Chapter 3

Havoc: A man, crippled from birth, is healed completely.

Power: Two men, on their way to prayer, who are a part of a continuing prayer program, declare deliverance in Jesus' name.

Chapter 4

Havoc: Multitudes experience reconciling peace and joy, in contrast to the usual turmoil and emptiness of world-life, and a practical pattern of caring for the needy evolves.

Power: A small group of believers-in-Jesus, censured by religionists who command them to be silent, get down to earnest prayer. The earnestness of the prayer results in a shake-up and a refilling of the Holy Spirit life-flow.

Chapter 5

Havoc: Hypocrisy seeking to invade the community of believers is tended to by holy judgment. Two people die of heart failure. Strangely, this purification results in believers being "the more added to the Lord, multitudes of both men and women."

Power: Praying leadership operates humbly yet boldly in the discernment the Holy Spirit gives.

Chapter 5

Havoc: Sick folk are healed, invalids recover, mental cases are restored and demons cast out.

Power: People are continuing to gather "in one accord" at their regular meeting place.

Chapter 5

Havoc: Believers, put in prison for making people well, are released during the night by an angelic visitation. Religious leaders, confounded by this, capture the escapees who, strangely enough, haven't run but are back in the temple grounds declaring life to all. They are beaten, and puzzle their punishers by refusing to show animosity or bitterness for their treatment.

Power: A pathway of praise and rejoicing, worship and trust in God's overruling working, releases people from the usual order of fear, intimidation, bitterness or retaliation.

Chapter 6

Havoc: Great wonders and miracles are performed by the power of the Holy Spirit, and Stephen's ministry is labeled blasphemous.

Power: The leadership of the church is committed to "prayer and the ministry of the Word."

Chapters 7 and 9

Havoc: Under the leadership of Saul of Tarsus, Stephen is stoned, but Saul will later be converted en route to Damascus.

Power: Stephen dies praying, rendering forgiveness in the face of his accusers.

The book recounts one case after another of havoc worked by righteousness—the *right*-ness of God's working—which evicts the unrighteousness of sickness, suffering, sin, hypocrisy, death and destruction. On every page we see that one thing begets the power which wreaks such havoc in the world of the bound: Prayer.

Prayer in response to an appointment by the Lord.

Prayer as a corporate response to a crisis.

Prayer as a daily practice.

Prayer as a point of praiseful rejoicing.

Prayer as an expression of worship.

Prayer as a simple utterance spoken by but one in a time of need.

Prayer. Prayer. Prayer.

The Book of Acts develops its report. Moving outside the region of Jewry, where religiousness was at the root of the deadness, the early Christians meet other forms of living death. By prayer they release God's power and invade the world of paganism, of satanic worship through occultism, of superstition and intellectualism.

They come to Europe and at Philippi confront a demon in a fortuneteller. For driving out that spirit in the name of Jesus Christ, Paul and Silas are accused of "troubling the city."

In Athens, Paul sees, in the midst of enormous intellectual sophistication, superstition to the extent that every corner has a shrine to some god. In fact the Athenians were so afraid of omitting an unknown deity that they had built a shrine to it.

For simply but powerfully stating that there is one God Almighty above all, and that all men are responsible to Him as His creatures, Paul is derided and mocked.

In Ephesus, people turned away in droves from the worship of the pagan idol Artemis. They burned thousands of dollars worth of their own occult literature as a token of their conversion.

The local merchants, notably the silversmiths who fashioned statues of Artemis, responded viciously. A riot ensued, indicative of the level of sanity and reason which Satan employs to fight the encroachment of righteousness into his realm.

The invasion is always preceded by prayer, sustained by prayer and accomplished with prayer. And it is an invasion. There is nothing tame about it. Nothing short of a violent "turning upside down" accomplishes the objective of the King. His violent death on the cross lit the fuse to this explosion destined to drive hell out of earth and back within its own boundaries.

The church was just learning. Its prayer power was developing forms of expression, and through a study of the Word those instruments of power may be taken in hand to this day.

And we need them today.

The battle not only isn't over, but it is raging with a heretofore unknown intensity. Small wonder, then, that the Holy Spirit is moving across the earth to raise up a people of prayer. "For the eyes of the Lord run to and fro throughout the whole earth, to shew himself strong in behalf of them whose heart is perfect toward him" (II Chronicles 16:9).

Two threads of truth begin to converge:

1. There are patterns of prayer that not only may be observed but also learned as instruments of battle to extend the kingdom of our God.

2. The rising intensity of evil in our world, and the rising of a new work of the Holy Spirit in the church, may indicate that a distinctly significant season of battle is upon us.

God never intended the Bible to be a museum wherein past triumphs of faith might be examined for their historical interest. Rather, "Seeing we are compassed about with so great a cloud of witnesses, let us run with patience the race set before us."

The Acts show us believers who invaded the impossible. The study reveals anything but a mild kind of prayer. They prayed, then commanded cripples to walk. They prayed, then the place where they were was shaken. They prayed, and then marched into a pagan world with truth. One prayed forgiveness, as blood streamed from his stone-torn wounds.

Violence.

Life breaking into the strongholds of death.

Light driving darkness into the corners.

Love.

Love without gushiness.

Love without fear.

Loving violence. Violent lovingness.

It won once, in a world stormed over with darkness.

It right-side-upped a world upside-down.

It can again.

But it will require some participants who understand love
. . . and the violence involved in prayer which extends it.

It will require recruits who will learn the skills of spiritual battle, and who will let the Holy Spirit make them bold enough to employ them.

Even if a few end up like Stephen.

Any takers?

*There is no neat way to deliver life. Beware
of well-wrapped and beautifully beribboned
packages which claim to contain it.*

7.
THE VIOLENCE OF LOVE

All this talk of violence may trouble some. That Jesus said, "The kingdom of God is allowing for violence, and the violent are breaking in," registers with few. That hell is enlarging itself, and that the whole world lies in the evil one are facts that seem only theological in significance. To many believers, that Christ died to save sinners usually only means that if they receive God's forgiveness through the Lord Jesus Christ they can go to heaven some day.

Of course, that's true.

But Jesus' teaching ministry was not aimed at showing people they were sinners and headed for hell unless they got saved. It was not a soul-winning course in teaching men ways to secure decisions from the unconverted. Rather, He incessantly taught the truth of a kingdom—the kingdom of God—which was presented as a dynamic force prepared to enter the human scene *now*. Jesus was not a "sweet by and by" preacher.

He did promise us a dwelling place with Him, and He did teach of rewards for those who serve His purpose faithfully.

But His ministry was much about violence.

"I came not to bring peace, but a sword." He interprets that in another place, when Peter takes an actual sword as an instrument of self-defense: "Put it away," Jesus directs. "My kingdom doesn't win with the use of swords." The weapons of the battle are not of iron and steel. They are spiritual instruments. But they are for war.

Don't think either of Jesus' mission *or* ours as being placid. Peace of heart, mind and soul are our portion. But from this deeply settled certainty of spirit, we are to move into conflict.

"I send you forth as sheep among wolves."

"Rejoice when men persecute and revile you for my name's sake. So persecuted they the prophets which were before you."

"They shall deliver you up to be afflicted and shall kill you: and ye shall be hated of all nations for my name's sake."

"Behold, I give unto you power to tread on serpents and scorpions, and over all the power of the enemy."

"Because you are not of the world, but I have chosen you out of the world, therefore, the world hates you."

No one in history manifested more love than did Jesus. He patiently ministered with compassion to crowds of sick and tormented people. He labored to the point of exhaustion to allay human need. Little children wanted to be near Him. He readily forgave social outcasts and sinners who sought Him . . . or who were thrown by brutal hands before Him. He wept for mankind, hopeless before death's door. He tenderly lamented the plight of the Holy City which had unwittingly sealed its own doom by rejecting Him.

But there is another side.

His eyes burn with anger against religious bigots who would

rather see a man remain deformed than violate their traditions. His hand brandishes a whip and He sends tables sprawling with coins and animals scattered like leaves before a storm, as He rejects religious commercialism. He casts demons out of a wreck-of-a-human, deeming the recovery of one man to be worth more than the price of a herd of hogs. He is conscious His words are exciting such venomous hatred in His opponents that they are plotting His murder, yet He doesn't let up.

He summons us toward learning a balance.

To see both sides of Jesus is to see both sides of prayer. It is to see the need for compassion, for care, for concern, for weeping with those that weep, for sympathy, for groaning, for aching deeply because of what you sense transpiring in human lives. And it is to learn the place and time for anger, when we see Satan's wiles successfully destroying; for indignation, when the adversary's program violates territory that is rightfully Christ's; for boldness, when demonic hordes announce their presence; for attack, when the Holy Spirit prompts an advance which faith can make but before which our flesh quails.

Violence and love are not contradictory.

A poisonous snake in a child's crib would bring a violent reaction from a parent. An intruder into a home is met with hostility. An alien with ill intent will find no hospitality or asylum within a nation. The love of child, home and nation argue against violence and love being contradictory. Common sense resolves the contradiction.

So does spiritual sense.

The serpent has crawled into man's earth. The Father has willed the crushing of his head. The universal intruder sought to usurp the throne of heaven's home and was cast down to hell. We are told to perform the same "casting down" whenever we discover him yet "boasting" himself against God. The alien does not belong on this planet, but because so many entertain his presence, he is yet able to resist the purpose of God. Until the day of Jesus Christ, however, we must effectively and successfully confront his workings: "Resist the devil and he will flee from you."

However, any who have ever confronted his operations know that it is not a task for the mild-mannered. Neither the fanciful nor the fanatic will succeed. Dreamy, misty-eyed optimism or wild-flailing, shrieking emotionalism will produce nothing.

But redeemed men and women whose hearts are filled with love, and who resist indignantly the slings of hell not only can enter the battle—they will win in it.

In every sense, Calvary broke the serpent's back. The cross holds the ultimate declaration of victory: "It is finished." Yet the outworking of its power awaits applicants for its ministry.

But they must learn of Calvary's power.

Love.

And, they must also learn Calvary's price.

Violence.

PART TWO

*. . . and they
continued stedfast
in prayers . . .*

8.
REPROGRAMING THE FREED

Prayer is not a piece of antique religious furniture to be displayed on special occasions like an ornament. Nor is it a matter of spiritual guesswork by which a holy roll of the heavenly dice is made to see if you might strike it rich; a kind of godly gamble, hoping against the apparently inevitable.

That kind of thinking has a name.

Snake eyes.

Satan, the serpent, has hypnotized most of mankind with an astonishingly complex set of ideas hindering prayer. Knowing, as he does, that only praying people can break his coiled death grip on the planet, he has breathed concept after concept into the framework of human thought. These concepts dominate all those who still live under the control of and within the structures of that destroyer's order of things.

However, Jesus has pioneered a new race.

From among the moving dead, He has called to himself all who will join Him in life. All are welcome to answer His invitation to live—a possibility He made available when He broke the death trap by succumbing voluntarily to it.

And then rising again.

They are the freed, these who answer His call. And it is His life in them that makes possible their experience of love, joy and peace. But more, His life in each of them inevitably threatens the present system. The freed may also become the freers.

Life is dangerously present. They are communicators of it. They have the resident capacity to transmit it wherever they will.

Prayer is the basic pattern of transmission. If they learn to employ it, life will continually overwhelm the forces of death.

But most of the freed, formerly hypnotized by the wisdom of the snake, have emerged from their trance with a residue of his directives seemingly controlling much of their behavior. Like people carrying out posthypnotic suggestions fed them during the period of their trance, large numbers of believers hold spurious ideas about prayer.

Their new birth in Jesus the Lord has brought life. But His light seems to penetrate the mind only gradually. Boldness does not come quickly, but only as the freed learn the truth. "You shall know the truth, and the truth shall make you free" (John 8:32).

Ongoing patterns of discovery, then, are needful—a constant challenging of old patterns of thought through growth in the truth, a casting down of world-mindedness. These break the enchantment of the serpent's stare. They explode the instructions programed in our minds during the time we walked according to the persisting disorder of things.

In this section, having already acknowledged the power of prayer and recognized it as an instrument of violence against evil, we will try to overcome the ideas that limit actual praying. Hindrances abound, all the way from the supposition that prayer effectiveness is a rare gift available only to the uniquely holy, to the false idea that prayer is a kind of cosmic game in which you try to tune in to the predestined design of things.

Ignorance is rampant, even among the enlightened.

Bondage straps minds, even among the freed.

There are power-releasing truths to be discovered. Truths which will become implemented as keys, as the freed become the freers. The middle step—becoming increasingly "freed-up"—awaits us.

9.
THE PRIMER ON PRAYER

Probably nothing hinders an attitude of expectancy in prayer more than the supposition that all effective prayer has to take a long time. Inherent in our nature is the conviction that, to get anything from God, we have to work hard to earn it. Most of us are at least superficially convinced that it all hangs on God's grace, that we can be forgiven solely by free favor shown through the Lord Jesus Christ. But, beyond that beginning, even the sincerest person will still be much inclined to believe that great prayer requires great amounts of time.

The stories of powerful men and women, who have prayed and shaped lives and nations through hours of intercession and lengthy travail, seem to buttress the case against my being effective in prayer.

But Jesus taught a pathway to development in praying that anyone of us can walk. It may lead eventually to experiences like those of the great pray-ers whose dedication so intimidates us. But their arrival at those heights began with early steps on the flat lands where they learned basic attitudes toward prayer—and, no doubt, where they cast off many false notions

53

about it as well. Let us begin in the same way.

Jesus once told a story (see Luke 11:1-13) which ought to be the primer on prayer. That story tells us that God wants us to ask Him freely and boldly for whatever we need. Ironically, however, its original intention has been seriously distorted. The principal reason for this is one word in verse 8: importunity.

Importunity appears in the King James Version, while persistence is the unfortunate translation in most modern versions. Perhaps the best way to discover the simple power of what Jesus was unfolding in His preliminary teaching on prayer is to retell the story:

"Suppose a friend of yours arrives at your house in the middle of the night, after traveling all day long. Because he hasn't had anything to eat, you go to prepare something for him, only to discover that your pantry is empty.

"Because the shops are closed at that hour, you decide to go to the nearby home of another friend, and, although it's a horrible time to arouse anyone, bang loudly on the door.

"Now answer me," Jesus is saying, "which of you has a friend who would stand at his bedroom window and shout out to you saying, 'Don't bother me. The whole household's in bed'?

"Of course not! It's not even a question of friendship. The man will get up and give him what he needs because of the simple fact that the neighbor had the nerve to ask.

"And I'm telling you—*ask*, and it shall be given unto you!"

That's the uncluttered version of Jesus' story. It tells how to learn to pray well. To begin, you need to learn to have the nerve to ask boldly.

A look at the original language supports this simple approach, so much so that it is mind-boggling to understand why this passage has been used to show that prayer must earn answers through overcoming God's reluctance, as if our persistence could overcome God's resistance.

In fact, Jesus is saying, "Your first barrier isn't God—it's your own hesitance to ask freely. You need to learn the kind of boldness that isn't afraid to ask—whatever the need or the circumstance."

The lesson revolves around one idea: shameless boldness. The word employed here occurs only twice in the Greek New Testament, once in its positive form and once in its negated form. In I Timothy 2:9 *aidos* is used to describe a posture of propriety and reverence. It means "modesty" or "respect." It applies to the adornment of women that should distinguish them from the brassiness of the worldly woman. The Elizabethan English word "shamefacedness," which appears in the King James Version, is literally correct but its flavor has changed too much in 350 years to be helpful any longer, when it comes to ladies' garments.

But Jesus' use of the word in this parable is in its negated form—*anaideia*. The "alpha privitive" of the Greek language has the same force as English prefixes like "im" or "un." Negated, "possible" becomes "*im*-possible"; "likely" becomes "*un*-likely."

And Jesus said the reason the midnight seeker gets what he needs is because of his *anaideia*—not his reverence, not his modest sensitivity to the hour, not his caution, nor his respect for propriety, but his bold unashamedness—indeed, his *brassiness*.

It isn't the brassiness of a smart aleck making demands, but the forwardness of a person who is so taken with an awareness of need that he abandons normal protocol.

There is nothing in the text that lends itself to the idea of persistence. The contrast is clear: the awakened friend gets up and gets what is needed. He doesn't carry on a war of words from the upstairs window. Nor does he smolder silently in irritation under the blankets while his friend downstairs insistently beats the door and shouts his need into the unresponding darkness.

The only other point of confusion lies in a misunderstanding of the verb "ask." Its tense in Greek conveys the idea of continual asking. But that is not a command to ask repeatedly for the same thing in order to force God into action. The continuality which Jesus wants is in ceaseless petitioning. In other words, you need never hesitate to ask for something just because you asked for something else earlier. Any hint that heaven "gets too busy" with earlier requests to have either time or supply for the next is pure folly.

Here's the message of the parable:

1. You have a *friend* in the heavenly Father. He's on your side, and available anytime, in every circumstance.

2. Boldness is your privilege. Your assignment is to *ask*; His commitment is to *give*—as much as you need.

This is the beginning. "Seeking" and "knocking" are further steps as one walks the pathway of prayer. But we need to get started, and this is probably the greatest need facing us today: too many hesitate to pray. They hesitate through a sense of unworthiness, a feeling of distance from deity, a wondering about God's will in the matter, a concern over "if it's okay," an uncertainty of how *much* to ask for, a fear that God won't hear.

Jesus strikes the death blow to such hesitancy: *ask*. Ask with unabashed forwardness; ask with shameless boldness! He commands. And when you do, He clearly teaches, "your friend, my Father, will rise to the occasion, and see that everything you need is provided."

Father, forgive me for ignorantly doubting your willingness or your readiness to help me, as my friend.

Please release me from the trap which fear has snapped on

my mind, pinching my faith down to the size of my limited imaginings about your great goodness.

Thank you for receiving me as I begin my best lessons in prayer with this one. I need not ever be ashamed to ask you anything. *Amen.*

10.
IF WE DON'T, HE WON'T

Listen to words often spoken which reflect our distorted views of prayer:

1. "We've tried everything else. I guess we'll have to pray and hope God does something."

2. "Chuck and Cindy's baby is okay now. Somebody said they had phoned a church to pray for him. He probably would have gotten better anyhow."

3. "I certainly would like to see things happen in our family, but . . . well, I guess God knows best. We'll just hope everything works out all right."

4. "No, Susan, the big order was canceled. That does it. Drops the bottom out of the business. We're sunk. Only a miracle can save us now."

5. "Oh, sure, I've wanted more spiritual strength in my life. In fact, I would like the Lord to fill me with His Spirit. Whenever He thinks I'm ready, I suppose He'll do it."

6. "Dear, daddy is sick and the doctor says he might di . . . , uh, have to go to be with Jesus. So we have to just trust God if that's what He wants for daddy and us."

7. "Oh, God, we don't know why this has happened, but we ask for the ability to accept things as they are."

These are a full round of examples of human ignorance. Please note the word is ignorance, not stupidity. Ignorance is a commentary on what we don't know, stupidity on what we don't *do*. Our prayerlessness could be called stupid, if the inaction did not derive from an amazing failure to understand God's attitude about prayer.

Knowing His attitude will determine ours. No one would intentionally buy into a defunct business or try to solve an impossible equation. If prayer is a wild goose chase, then let's forget it.

If the seven quotations above accurately reflect our attitudes about prayer, then we would have to conclude that God runs a sloppy operation. No wonder people don't pray.

Prayer ends up as a last-ditch option, a maybe-it'll-work-and-maybe-it-won't proposition, an expression of resignation to fate, an assignment of blame to the creator, a mild statement about the fact-of-God. The quotes show that we regard God as one who:

1. Is sometimes available, but only after you have done your best first.

2. Is lucky to have circumstances support His program at given points.

3. Is sitting in heaven knowing things which He may or may not tell someone.

4. Is hopefully tuned in when a human pratfall squashes the panic button.

5. Stands with a heavenly stopwatch, waiting for a mystery moment when He will spring some nifty surprise.

6. Omnisciently drops disasters on and deals heartrending tragedy to whomever He wills, because He knows that's better for you.

7. Can't do any more about circumstances than you can, but can help you feel better about them.

Who needs it? The only reason to bother is to propitiate a God who taunts, not to reverence the One who triumphs. Recognize Him cautiously lest you incite His wrath, but don't expect anything from Him except maybe an annual lucky day.

We need to repent. Repentance in the classical sense means gaining a new mentality. We might do better to define repent by saying, "Get your head on straight!"

Let's get three things straight:

First, God is a good God.

Second, sin and Satan—flesh and hell—have fouled up God's intended processes for mankind.

Third, the redeemed—those who have received God's gift of life in Jesus—are the main channel of His dealing in grace and goodness on this planet.

The image of a frowning God, brooding in anger and perched on the edge of a ten-mile-high cliff with a quiver of lightning bolts ready for hurling at the unsuspecting and the helpless, must be smashed. The beauty of the Father's personality was so perfectly mirrored in Jesus himself, that, the Savior declares, "If you've seen me, you've seen the Father" (John 14:9). The combination of His compassion for the victims of human dilemma and His triumph over each dilemma He encounters, furnishes us with a stamp of God's image: God is good. God does good. He cannot even be tempted to do otherwise (James 1:13).

I Timothy 1:11 speaks of "the glorious gospel of the blessed God." The word blessed (*makarios*) also means happy. The good news of the gospel which the early church spread was that there was a God unlike the pagan deities, who plagued man with tragic trickery, or at whose hand "happiest" moments of sexual indulgence or drunken revelry were always exchanged for eventual disappointment and despair. "The blessed God" He is called—one who is bent on man's fulfillment and happiness.

"God is love" is not an old saw, it is a biblical affirmation (I John 4:8). It does not depersonalize the Almighty by replacing Him with an idea or an emotion. To the contrary, it defines His nature. "God is love" says that anything and everything which answers to the finest qualities of true love flows from Him. He is the source of all real love. He is also the judge of all that would call itself love and by its counterfeit seek to deceive minds and destroy hearts.

Let it be once and forever settled: "Every good gift and every perfect gift is from above, and cometh down from the Father of lights, with whom is no variableness, neither shadow of turning" (James 1:17).

Secondly, the multiplicity of things which wring the joy out of life do not proceed from God. They are the result of a fallen race reaping the harvest of its own sowing, accented by specific operations of the prince of evil. The Book of Job, so often referred to by the fearful or the cynical as proof of God's commitment to destroy happy homes and clobber healthy bodies, is in reality an explanation of Satan's commitment to deprive man of all that is fulfilling to him. He is clearly the one seeking to steal, to kill and to destroy. And that is what Jesus said of him, in calling him the thief (John 10:10).

With the accents of the adversary's workings, there is the self-inflicted turmoil we heap upon ourselves by ignorance of and rebellion against spiritual laws. The law of sowing and reaping (Galatians 6:7,8) is as certain as the law of gravity. Much of that for which mankind indicts God as unkind is the simple harvest of man's own folly. The whole purpose of God's commands is to warn against the destructive power of sin, not to badger man with a landlocking set of rules which would take the wind out of full sail living. "For this is the love of God, that we keep his commandments: and his commandments are not grievous" (I John 5:3). Carnal violation of healthy order produces confusion.

Sin and Satan work disorder and destruction. God doesn't. He shows the way to surmount our own propensity for failure and heartbreak, and to overcome the slings of satanic fury bent on death and destruction.

Thirdly, you and I can help decide which of these two things—blessing or cursing—happens on earth. We will determine whether God's goodness is released toward specific situations or whether the power of sin and Satan is permitted to prevail.

Prayer is the determining factor.

But the problem is that too few want to accept the fact that if we don't pray, He won't do anything.

This issue presents more than just a problem, it breeds a controversy—the long-term debate between human responsibility and divine sovereignty. To some, an emphasis on the responsibility of man suggests that eternal issues are sacrificed on the altar of man's obvious imperfection. To others, an emphasis on divine sovereignty suggests a deterministic universe in which God's will irresistibly makes everything happen. Too much of human responsibility produces an erratic world; too much of divine sovereignty a fatalistic one.

We will not solve this question, but there is no way to come to terms with our responsibility without acknowledging the issue. Man is completely disinclined to accept his God-given responsibility. God hasn't given man charge of the universe, but He did give man charge of this planet. And the current disorder of things is man's problem.

Since only the white light of Calvary's power can dissipate the black workings of hell, the only people who can change bleak circumstances and reverse the tide of encroaching evil wherever it rises are those who pray in Jesus' name.

But sloth is the earmark of Adam's race when it comes to spiritual responsibility. We would rather blame God than trust Him; rather complain about Him than call upon Him. How many would rather indict the Almighty for neglect when hell comes against us, than invite His almightiness to eject the hell-worker?

Jesus said to pray: "Father, we invite your ruling might to overrule what's happening here. Do your will and cast out that which opposes your will." Those words are the essence of what we have recited so many times, "Thy kingdom come, thy will be done on earth as it is in heaven."

Christ has solemnly charged us, "It's up to you. If heaven's will and power are to be worked on earth, you have to ask for it." He removes the guesswork from answering the question, "Who's responsible?"

Man is.

I am.

You are.

If hell or failing flesh win, it's because no one withstands the fire or the foolishness. The Lord Jesus' instructions to "Ask . . . Seek . . . Knock" contain a combination which is intended to unlock the shackles of hopelessness.

Ask—call on God to work in the midst of those circumstances where sin or Satan is succeeding.

Seek—pursue the path He opens, knowing He will lead you to discover the underlying structure of the circumstance; discover its foundation, discern its root.

Knock—strike the obstacle, like the friend knocking at the door who overcame the only obstacle between him and provision for his need (Luke 11:5-10), like the widow who stayed at the unjust judge's door, striking the object that was shut up against justice being served (Luke 18:1-8), like the apostle who directed the church to pray in order that hindrances to effective ministry be crumbled (Colossians 4:2, 3).

John Wesley said, "God will do nothing on earth except in answer to believing prayer." In honor of His own Son who died to make possible the full invasion of His almighty power into the impossibilities of earth, God will do nothing apart from the people His Son has redeemed. Jesus urged that we pray for the entrance of the Father's kingdom power in all situations. He urged that we not succumb to the fears that argue for surrender to earth or hell's worst . . . or their least. We are simply not to tolerate that which diminishes, demeans, distresses or destroys. *Instead:*

"Seek first God's kingdom, and all these things shall become a plus!"

"Don't be afraid, little flock, it is the Father's delight to make a gift to you of His overruling power." (See Luke 12:31, 32.)

He still holds to His original proposition: "Man is in charge on earth. If hell is allowed to take over, or if the flesh fumbles the ball, it's man's duty to call upon me for the remedy. If he doesn't call—if prayer isn't uttered—I have bound myself not to be involved. If prayer is extended, I have bound myself to conquer everything that would destroy or diminish my beloved creature, man."

There it is.

Prayer can change anything. The impossible doesn't exist.

His is the power.

Ours is the prayer.

Without Him, we cannot.

Without us, He will not.

Father, thank you for stretching me to become a responsible, maturing child of yours. I feel your longing to invade earth with your kingdom's love and power. Forgive me where I have doubted your readiness or almightiness to overrule the effects of sin.

Mighty Lord, I embrace the truth which is freeing me from my sense of helplessness and bringing me to a sense of true authority in prayer. I ask you, Holy Spirit, to grant me boldness to withstand through prayer those destructive forces opposed to your loving plan. Believing the promise and privilege are mine, I accept the responsibility of prayer at this new dimension.

Thine is the kingdom, the power and the glory.

In Jesus' Name. *Amen.*

11.
THE SYNDROME OF SILENCE

Few things stifle prayer more than the fact that, too often, we don't know what to pray for. We are hesitant to ask for something that we're not sure if we should have; to request God's action when we feel we lack the facts; to pray, for fear that our request may run crosscurrent to God's intended plan. The solution is simple: God's will is that we ask. Solving what His will is isn't my problem. Nonetheless, many are afraid to make certain petitions with confidence, for fear they may be asking out of order. Let's analyze this.

First, God's will is that we pray. "Ask, and keep on asking," Jesus commanded. The hearing heart and all-wise mind of the Father are not components in some heavenly computer that might blow a fuse if we ask too often. Heaven's storehouse is not a center that periodically is in short supply, and which we must guard by being careful to ask with appropriate reserve. God isn't rationing answers to prayer as though there was a shortage on His ability to beget, provide, heal or produce. Let's settle it: He's the creator. When you're dealing with the source of all things, nothing is a problem.

I was attending a small prayer meeting when someone suggested we pray for the healing of a back condition suffered by one of the other participants in the group. This request prompted a lady there to ask that we pray for an absent friend who had a similar back condition. To this, the one whose back problem had been mentioned first responded: "Oh, yes. I know about their pain [referring to the second case mentioned]. Don't bother praying for me. Their case is much worse than mine. Let's pray for them."

Laughable.

Or is it cry-able?

What on the surface appeared to be a compassionate remark was in actuality a humorously pathetic commentary on the view some have of God's capacity for answering prayer. It was as if the Almighty only has so many gifts to pass out, and when the supply is exhausted, it's "tough luck for the latecomers."

"The Lord's hand is not shortened, that it cannot save; neither his ear heavy, that it cannot hear" (Isaiah 59:1). That ought to settle the case. When the question rises, "Is it okay to pray this prayer?", let the answer be once and forever settled: Yes, it's okay. How? Just ask!

We worry about knowing exactly what to pray in some cases because we think we know what to pray in all others. We may, at times. But aren't there many times that we have asked imperfectly? God was not befuddled. Our ignorance did not clog the wheels of the universe.

When we are uncertain as to how boldly we may ask, we are saying, "I'm afraid to ask for this because I might confuse the Almighty. I may just force His hand to violate His own eternal purposes, and suddenly bring our world to a screeching halt when my mightiness of faith has secured an answer on earth which God didn't really want to give." It is as though we somehow think a cosmic accident might occur if we invade

68

heaven with a request that would somehow slip through the machinery of providence without being checked out carefully. Somehow God would find himself awkwardly glancing toward earth wondering, "How did I ever let that happen. I must be more careful about my answers to prayer."

"But," you ask, "what if my request isn't appropriate to God's will? What if I am asking for something that I shouldn't?"

The discovery of God's perfect will won't happen by excursions of human reason, assertions of man-made theology or personal opinions about "how I think God does or ought to do things." To the contrary, the Bible tells us how to discover His will through praying, not how to find His will and then pray.

"I implore you, brothers and sisters: present yourselves before God in a posture of worship; the kind that God accepts. It's the only truly intelligent thing you can do. Therein you will find a transforming of your mentality from the world-way of thinking to God's new way for you; and therein you will discover the whole counsel of His perfect will" (Romans 12:1, 2, paraphrase).

When we don't know what liberty we have in requesting, we should come with worship and ask everything our hearts long to ask, or that with which our minds are preoccupied. Then, maintain a heartfelt stance of worship before the omniscience—all-knowingness—of His counsel and purposes. You can be sure of one thing: He won't mock or criticize you for asking. "If any man lack wisdom (i.e., in this case, the certainty of what we ought to or can ask for), let him ask of God, who gives to all men liberally, and doesn't rebuke you for asking" (James 1:5).

Naturally, we wonder, "But what if the answer to my prayer is no?"

There is no such thing as a no answer. That is not to say that

God responds to either our whims or our mistaken requests. There is a battery of Scriptures that make clear that some prayers will not be answered:

1. Prayers of self-indulgence will not be answered. James 4:2, 3.

2. Presumptuous attitudes in prayer will not be honored. Luke 9:51-56.

3. Prayer offered from a heart which simultaneously calculates disobedience will not even be heard. Psalm 66:18.

4. Mouthing prayer while tolerating unforgiveness toward others blocks the provision of even our most basic needs. Matthew 6:11, 12.

But the individual who wants to invade impossibilities will be prepared to be honest with God. I don't have to be all-knowing, I don't have to have arrived at some special level of holiness, I don't need a record of great accomplishments of faith.

But I do need to be honest, straightforward, open.

"If you abide in me, and my words abide in you [if you relate without guile and are receptive to what I'm teaching you along the way], *you shall ask what you will, and it shall be done unto you*" (John 15:7).

Uncanny.

Absolutely unbelievable.

Except, He said it—ask what *you* will.

And after all, He didn't sacrifice one iota of His own integrity by making that promise, because it's predicated on a significant premise: abiding in Him. That isn't a mystical position or some hard-to-arrive-at pattern of conduct. It isn't a religious accomplishment or a pious performance. It's just honest-to-God saying, "I want your will."

His answer: "Pray, and I'll work it."

Let's get on with the program and stop asking questions.

70

Dear Lord God,

How truly wonderful you are.

I kneel to marvel at the simplicity of your program for mankind.

I rejoice because your will is not beyond my discovery. I falsely judged your readiness to reveal yourself. Forgive me, I pray.

I want to learn how to discover your will by bold petition at your throne.

Already my heart is happy, knowing that, as I am seeking your will, I am by that very act performing it.

Praise Your Name! *Amen.*

12.
DIRTY LINEN IN THE THRONE ROOM

Honesty is indeed a prerequisite to effective prayer. But it can also be cleverly guided on a boomerang path by our arch opponent.

"How can I pray when I *know* I've failed God?" I may ask myself. The awareness of recent sin or even a remote memory can haunt the mind and cripple all confidence in prayer.

Further, I will never feel guilt but that Satan, whom God's Word labels as the accuser as well as the adversary, will hound my mind with added evidence of my unworthiness and, therefore, of my hopelessness if I do pray.

"You've botched it up so badly, how can you seriously expect a hearing from God. You don't deserve anything. You know it, and He knows it! Forget it!"

Some of us will even press beyond that lying attack to the point of praying something, somehow, but the words—when the mind is bombarded by guilt and condemnation—have a way of falling to the floor. Absent is that sense of the creative power when we speak boldly in simple trust to the God of all the heavens. We feel instead like someone who seeks an audience with the head of state of a nation whose flag we have just trampled.

Fat chance of a favor!

Thin hope of a hearing!

The devil's right. Forget it.

But wait a minute.

Think clearly for a moment. What suddenly changed Satan's nature that he would defend God's glory by urging you to keep your dirty distance?

Nothing.

He's consistently opposed to my union and yours with the Father.

When the devil contests a believer on seemingly righteous grounds you can count on it that there's a trap in the system somewhere. Truth starts to surface. The God of all glory is also the God of all grace.

We need to learn how to handle our biggest obstacle to effective prayer: guilt—the sense of having failed and thereby being disqualified for bold approach.

How can I handle my dirty linen when I want to come to the throne room of the Almighty?

Sin is, on the face of it, an obstacle to communion with God. But, if we look more closely, we'll see that just the opposite is true because of Christ's sacrifice.

Consider:

1. My sin creates the possibility for His grace to abound.

2. My sin is a powerful reminder of my absolute dependence on Him.

3. My sin, when confessed, will occasion another display of His mercy.

4. My sin, when dealt with, brings me to the fountainhead of power: the cross, where Jesus' blood is found again to be eternally effective in dissolving bonds and releasing from guilt.

5. My sin, when forgiven, will defeat my adversary, who said I would be excluded from a hearing by reason of my failure. The Apostle Paul was actually accused of encouraging sin. It was untrue and he clearly denied the charge (Romans 3:8; 6:1, 2).

But it is understandable that the charge was made. For any correct teaching of God's infinite mercy has a way of sounding to the presumptuous like a license for sin. But we don't enter God's presence by presenting an admission card certifying our sinlessness. Nor does one stamp into the throne room with muddy feet and a glib, "Sorry about that."

A proper balance of humility and boldness is needed. Sin, by whatever description, cannot be skirted. Neither should sin be honored by allowing it to inhibit our praying.

Here's how to handle the problem:

First, understand God's posture. He's on the side of sinners. Jesus' critics puzzled that He was so frequently in the company of people who lacked religious pedigree and moral status: "This man companies with publicans and sinners!" The amazing thing was not only that He was willing to move among the sinful, but that He affected them and not the other way around.

God never condemns sinners, and He never condones sin. "My little children," John begins, "I am writing these things to you that you sin not" (I John 2:1). The message registers, and could produce a guilt feeling just by casual reading . . . except for the next sentence. "But if any man sin, we have one pleading our case before the Father—Jesus Christ, the righteous one. He is our sin-covering" (vss. 1-2). In other words, the Word of God says: "Absolutely, do not sin," then turns right around and says, "But when you do. . . ."

Although the heavenly Father does not hold a casual attitude toward sin, He is not shocked by it either. He has made provision for it, not as an invitation to sin, but to receive His

75

freedom from its guilt.

Second, we make a serious mistake if we think God's mercy is the result of some "smile-and-forget-it" bent in His nature. Humanistic theology features the Father as a somewhat doddering, near senile, harmless old man, who forgives because He couldn't do much else in His defense anyway. Or it says that God forgives whenever He is asked "simply because it's right and He ought to." It's a part of a gentlemen's agreement: we'll forgive God for letting the world go on in the generally messed up condition it is, if He will be fair about it and forgive us for those times we've contributed to the mess.

Most people never express such ideas or, for that matter, bother to discover what they do think about forgiveness. But to experience the full peace of forgiveness we must understand the key to its power.

God's forgiveness is available and adequate because it cost an infinite price: the blood of Jesus.

- Blood is the only price adequate to cover payment for sin (Hebrews 9:22).
- Jesus knew and announced that His death on the cross was that instrument of payment (Matthew 26:28).
- It was the Father's plan and the Son's agreement to this redeeming event that produced Calvary (Acts 2:23; Matthew 26:39).
- This message was foretold by the Old Testament prophets and confirmed by the preaching of the New Testament apostles (Isaiah 53:4-6; John 1:29; I Corinthians 15:3, I Peter 1:18,19).
- Both justification (acquittal for our sins) in the present and eternal blessing in the future are granted through the blood (Romans 5:9).
- Therefore, peace of mind and a clear conscience before God are available through the blood (Ephesians 2:13, 14;

Hebrews 9:14).

Forgiveness is abundant, but it isn't the splash of a supermarket display. It's the overflow of the cornucopia of His love designed to prompt our praise and thanksgiving. . . .

. . . and our bold approach to His throne, even when we have sinned.

That's the third point.

Handling dirty linen in the throne room is not accomplished by attempting to hide it, but by openly spreading it before God. That's what confession means: acknowledging exactly what we know to be so.

"If we confess our sins, he is faithful and just to forgive us our sins and to cleanse us from all unrighteousness" (I John 1:9).

"Let us therefore come boldly unto the throne of grace, that we may obtain mercy, and find grace to help in time of need" (Hebrews 4:16).

"In time of need." That's the time we are most encouraged to come. But when need arises—and is compounded by our own sense of sin and failure—that is the time we're least inclined to come boldly.

But it's the time we're most invited!

Has your desire to pray been blocked by a sense of guilt? Be done with that blockade!

Let the truth about the blood of Jesus, the truth about the Father's mercy, set you free!

I can come and be cleansed by the miracle of His creative working through the blood:

Purge me. . . and I shall be clean: wash me, and I shall be whiter than snow.

Create in me a clean heart, O God; and renew a right spirit within me (Psalm 51:7, 10).

Welcome to the throne room of heaven, sinner.

Come, be cleansed, and let your request be made known.

Loving Father God,
My heart is filled upon rethinking the greatness of your love and the completeness of your plan. I want to please you, but how often my flesh folds under the pressure of temptation.

I thank you that you know my frame, and you remember I am dust. And I thank you for the abundance of grace and the gift of your righteousness which you have made available to me through the cross of your Son.

In His name, and with faith in the power of His cleansing blood, I confess my specific points of failure which hinder bold belief in prayer. (Take time to specify those items which come to mind, then leave them once-and-for-all under the covenant of the blood.)

Thank you for receiving me, gracious Lord.

Amen.

13.
THE ONLY WAY TO FLY

Is Praise.

There is no other way to remain airborne.

Praise has been unlocked and freshly introduced over the past few years. Unfortunately, that's just long enough for people to learn how to talk about it even though few may truly understand much about it.

Every time the Holy Spirit brings refreshing to a certain truth, His people enjoy a first wave of joyous illumination. But before long the concept falls into casual conversation and the dynamic is lost.

Only short-lived victories are gained by those who do no more than *use* a truth. The secret of being truly set free by a truth is to *possess* it, and ultimately to become possessed by it. "The only way to fly" is not merely a clever slogan. You may "get off the ground" by being introduced to praise, but sustained flight will require a deeper understanding.

Three points of understanding will enhance the likelihood that your practice of praise will abide with you in wisdom: (1) distinguish between a pious habit and genuine obedience; (2)

dissect a recent development of the truth about praise to remove the error wrapped in it, and (3) discern the reason—the why and the how—that praise works.

First, praise isn't a set of hallelujah push-ups! Even good exercise can be pointless—it can even cause body tissue to deteriorate—if the body adapts to the given movement. What was once a challenge is no longer. What once built up now only wears down in a kind of erosion.

The same kind of thing happens with us and truth. The truth challenges us and we grow stronger through the ensuing conflict. In fact it actually produces desired results.

"It works!" And we tremble with a feeling of power. The invisible realm has yielded one of its secrets to an earnest soul.

And the newly acquired key smoothly unlocks door after door. Until, one day, it doesn't do anything.

Everything seems to stick.

The sure-fire, I-learned-it-and-I'm-not-gonna-forget-it key doesn't work. The concept has not become invalidated, but no spiritual reality will survive rote performance. Spirit is breath. But rote performance is an iron lung, methodical, dependable, making the right motions, but lifeless.

To pray effectively we must learn to praise God. "When you pray," Jesus began His teaching, "say, 'Our Father in heaven . . . Holy, holy, holy is your name.' "

Praise is right. "It is a good thing to give thanks unto the Lord" (Psalm 92:1).

Praise is lovely. "Praise is comely for the upright" (Psalm 33:1).

Praise is appropriate. "Thou art worthy, O Lord, for thou hast created all things" (Revelation 4:11).

Praise is happy. "Make a joyful noise unto the Lord, all the earth" (Psalm 98:4).

"Waiting upon the Lord," an expression that tends to sound

contemplative and introspective, is actually a summons to serve. Servants wait on their masters, and waiters serve customers. In praise you and I are directed toward faithful and powerful service. Praise announces our entry into His presence, purifies our attitude and insures our fulfillment while we learn to wait in His presence.

But the perfunctory performance of praise, even as an act of obedience to the Scriptures quoted, can result in a legalistic loyalty devoid of power. Worship is to be "in spirit" as well as "in truth" (John 4:24). The truth about praise is already clearly taught by scores of excellent writings, and definitively required in the Word of God. Two other points require discussion.

1. Praise as it relates to difficulty, trial and tragedy.
2. The reason praise works.

"In every thing give thanks: for this is the will of God in Christ Jesus concerning you" (I Thessalonians 5:18). That verse first found its way with power into our home through trouble. Our first three children were born within a four- and-one-half-year span. Then seven years elapsed. We thought our family was ordained to be numbered at five. Our fiscal balance as a young couple was beginning to stabilize. The kids were all in school, and Anna had more time for personal interests and activities.

Then she became pregnant.

Most women can identify with the bewilderment of a "surprise" baby. Perhaps they haven't experienced it, but they can understand it.

"Lord," my wife prayed, "I don't mind having this child. I just want to be assured that this isn't some kind of 'parental accident' on our part. I don't believe in 'accidents,' Lord, but at a time like this I need a special assurance from you."

With the prayer on her lips, she did what some people would consider a peculiar thing. While neither of us advise folk to secure guidance in this manner, we do accept the fact that the Holy Spirit may well comfort hearts in the same way He did Anna's that day.

"Lord," she added, while standing at the kitchen sink, "I'm going to draw a promise from the promise box." She was referring to a small collection of about a hundred little cards with Scripture references on them. "I'm asking you to speak something very clearly to me by that means."

You can call it chance all you please. My wife and I know the Lord answered that prayer. The promise she drew?

"In every thing give thanks: for *this is the will of God* in Christ Jesus concerning you."

Her heart leapt!

And so did mine when she told me about it later that day.

"Honey, I feel as though the Lord personally told me that this baby is His will for us. Before that I could have accepted the fact and loved the baby, but now I can rejoice in the assurance and enjoy the pregnancy."

It's a preciously simple story.

And it shows how the Lord can use the Bible to say whatever He wants to one of His kids. People who force contextual rules of interpretation on simple promises the Holy Spirit breathes into human hearts violate the life of the Word. (I *don't* mean that interpretive rules are unimportant for teaching, but there ought to be a liberty when it comes to personalized promptings as God's Spirit speaks to individuals' hearts.) In fact the story includes a technical misinterpretation of the verse. God told Anna to praise Him because the pregnancy she questioned was His will for her. But—and it is a highly significant point—that is not what the verse says. And it is on the mistaken assumption that the verse does say that, that a bevy of questions has arisen.

The questions are based on the idea that every problem in life is somehow God's will for us and, therefore, He should be praised no matter how we feel or fail to understand what is happening to us. Questions like:

1. "Someone told me to praise God for everything that happens, and when we had the automobile accident I tried, but I couldn't seem to do it sincerely. Can you help me?"

2. "When I got sick I started praising God for it and nothing has happened. I can't seem to understand why He wants me to have this sickness. What do you think?"

3. "The baby died and I made up my mind I would praise God. What am I supposed to praise Him for—the death of my child?"

Those questions are not invented.

The verse does not say, "Everything that occurs is God's will in Christ Jesus concerning you, so give thanks for everything." It says instead: "In everything give thanks—for that very spirit of praise is God's will in Christ Jesus for you." In other words, the Word of God does not command us to thank God for every heartrending pain, evil, tragedy or trouble that crosses our path. Instead it tells us to never let circumstances dampen our praise.

And the verse does not say "for" everything give thanks, but "in" everything. Whatever the situation, irrespective how bleak, we are to praise God, but not for what He did to us, or for what He let happen, but that He is greater than the circumstance and that His love will guarantee our triumph over the test.

I believe this argument will stand in the face of Ephesians 5:20 which says we should thank God for all things. The word behind "for" in that verse is *huper* which is properly translated as "for" or "on behalf of." However its root meaning is "over" or "above." It has come into English in this sense as the prefix hyper-, as in hyperactive. Thus it is possible to construe Ephesians 5:20 to mean that our thanks should rise over all things, especially those things that trouble us.

This is different from the rote response to difficulty: "Well, I guess I'm supposed to praise God for this." To the contrary, it requires both faith and discernment. The faith is what prompts the praise:

1. Faith that His Word is true, and He will never forsake you (Matthew 28:20; Hebrews 13:5,6).

2. Faith that no obstacle can blockade your way interminably, nor any opponent defy God successfully (Luke 10:19; Psalm 108:13).

3. Faith that actually rejoices in the knowledge that victory is as certain as tomorrow and as verifiable as yesterday (Romans 8:37,39; II Corinthians 2:14).

The discernment is:

1. An ability to recognize that evil on this planet is not usually the will of the Father, but the result of man's disobedience that invites Satan's workings. At times, then, praise is to be joined with a retaliatory attack against recognized satanic operations.

2. The realization that we should mix with our praise bold affirmations of God's promises. These affirmations will begin working His unlimited power in the midst of whatever opposes us. Praise includes, then, honoring His Word which is always a creative word, for He is the creator.

Finally, we need to understand why praise "works." This understanding helps it cease to be a performed habit, like stroking a rabbit's foot, by which we hope to charm God into letting the heat off. There is a reason why praise is so powerful.

Praise is not psychological improvement of your attitude, as though God were saying, "Just buck up. Smile. Tell me I'm nice, and everything will seem nicer." God doesn't play "Grin and Bear It" with the victims of life's trials and tragedies.

Neither is praise the blind pursuit of heavenly intervention, as though our job is to stand on this side of a great cloud of unknowing, making cheerful sounds, and hoping to stir activity on the other side.

Praise is not intended to compliment God. Some people have confessed quite candidly in their more honest moments that they felt praise seemed like some effort to curry God's favor by soothing or massaging His heavenly ego.

What *is* it?

Praise is an instrument of violence.

Praise upsets the climate which furthers the growth of so much of life's suffering, confusion, turmoil and strife. Praise destroys the atmosphere in which sickness, defeat, discouragement and futility flourish. Praise beats out hell's brush fires. Praise breathes heaven's life into the vacuum death produces on earth. The consequent tornado of holy power will cast down the obstacles which sin, self, sickness and Satan have erected.

How does it work?

The quickest pathway to understanding praise is to study a profound statement made in Psalm 22:3, "But thou art holy, O thou that inhabitest the praises of Israel." This psalm is often called the psalm of the cross, because a thousand years before the occurrence, it prophesied several details of Jesus' death.

In essence, the psalm is declaring, "In spite of the hell that is breaking loose around me, to the extent that I feel forsaken by God, I still declare that you are entirely faithful (holy)." It is a psalm which affirms God's goodness while at the same time crying out for His presence.

Strange.

"Lord, I'm all alone. You don't even seem to be here. But I'm still saying, 'You're a good God.' "

An added statement keys us in on an understanding of why and how praise works. The answer lies in the word, "inhabitest." The Lord is revealed to "inhabit" the praises of Israel—and by "Israel" we clearly are dealing with any people who walk with Him according to the promises of His covenants. (Romans 9:6 and 2:29 make it clear that any Jew or Gentile who puts his faith in God's Messiah, Jesus, is in covenant relationship with the Almighty.)

Yawshab, the Hebrew verb which appears here, literally translates, "to sit down, to dwell or to remain." With reference to a king, it means "to be enthroned." God is enthroned upon the praises of His people.

Praise works because it reverses the prevailing rulership in an earthly situation. According to our earlier studies, all that plagues, torments and assails man is the outflow of the fall of man from God's ordained rule and the consequent usurping of earth-rule by Satan himself. As "prince of the power of the air," (Ephesians 2:2), he maintains the physical, spiritual, emotional and intellectual climate of earth at a temperature that is best for the kind of crop he seeks to harvest. His harvest is characterized by such things as discord, defeat, sickness, failure, poverty, division, bitterness, affliction, and the multitude of human ills and pains. When the fruit of his operations begins to be squeezed over your head, and the vicious outflow begins to engulf you, praise becomes the instrument of his defeat.

That's because praise lays a foundation for God's ruling power to descend upon—for His throne's rule and intent to dwell in the middle of our muddle. Praise makes a place for God's rule—His throne—to rest, and thereby begin to overrule the furies hell is working around us.

Praise is a human being saying:

God, you good Lord of goodness and blessed intent for me. What's happening does not reflect your nature. You are the author of life and peace, of health and blessing.

What's happening to me right now isn't like that, Lord, but I am calling on you. *Amen.*

PART THREE

. . . praying with all prayer
and supplication
in the spirit . . .

14.
PRAYING WITH ALL PRAYER

The summons to invade the impossible is not without accompanying instructions. The Bible tells us how prayer may be employed. Contrary to much general thought on the subject, prayer is not a push-button proposition—you did or you didn't. It is a multifaceted possibility, with a selection of means to prayer which deserve to be understood.

God is clearly seeking to cultivate a breed of maturing sons and daughters who understand something of His ways as well as who witness something of His acts. The evidence of the early church is that their patterns of life included "prayers"—not perfunctory religious ritual, but the natural life-flow of people who were learning ways to pray.

The plural of the word "prayer" in Acts 2:42 should not be misconstrued as the mere duplication of habit. Their "prayings" involved a growth in various applications of prayer practice which were suited to the occasion. Ephesians 6:18 says that the believer's participation as an invader of the impossible—standing in the spiritual struggle and making inroads on the workings of the adversary's dark kingdom—requires the use of "all prayer." We might call it all kinds of praying, at all times and by all means.

Those who understand the truth of "all prayer" are well equipped to undertake the toil of prayer. But we should never think that to know about prayer will take the place of prayer itself.

Prayer is essentially a partnership of the redeemed child of God working hand in hand with God toward the realization of His redemptive purposes on earth. This being so, there is no question that the Father's heart would have us understand something of the patterns of power He has made accessible to us.

Two joys await us:

(1) The joy of recognizing previous experiences which had remained undefined and uninterpreted.

(2) The joy of discovering realms of possibility which will release us toward new heights of prayer partnership with God.

Accordingly, then, in this section we study different facets of the praying life style. We will discover that prayer which invades the impossible does not increase without growth in our understanding. Efficient prayer does not require a knowledge of the mechanics of spiritual weaponry, but it is more quickly released—entered into—by such knowledge.

Part Three is more demanding reading than the first two parts. Exposition and examination are the elements of this section; the unfolding of Scripture content and the researching of significant themes which contribute to our understanding and exercise of prayer.

The newborn church in Acts 2 entered its first years of life with a stedfastness in "prayers." There had not been time to publish prayer books or manuals on prayer—even books about it. But they were growing in praying. Their established life style incorporated prayers—a plural noun.

We will begin where they did: with the prayer pattern Jesus taught them. In the following chapter, we seek to uncover the wonder of the most prayed prayer in the world—the Lord's Prayer.

Following that, a challenge to objectivity awaits some while a challenge to a holy adventure awaits all. The praying that irritates millions, the use of the supernatural language of prayer described in the Bible, is studied as a point of blessing and unity.

The ensuing two chapters on intercession and supplication are the fruit of one pastor's search for understanding as to why these different terms even existed. I was certain the Bible was not just dispensing synonyms for prayer, and was stirred to discover what I now share on these subjects. The concluding chapter discusses the beauty of balance.

Once we are sure that the impossible doesn't exist, a new problem arises.

There will be times when that monster doesn't yield to our assaults in prayer. There will be times when it does—quickly, suddenly—and we will savor the triumph.

But the problem of "why not always" is too often resolved by a timid move away from the bold declaration that "all things are possible." The loveliness of learning the sanity and symmetry of truth is that it will keep you free.

Free from cowardice when confronted by the impossible.

Free from having to answer every question when answers are not immediately forthcoming.

Free to acknowledge that however much we may learn, we will not learn everything in this lifetime.

Free to resist and reject doubt, and still have love and receptivity toward those who do.

Free to keep praying even when called foolish for doing so.

Free to believe . . . and to receive.

93

Free to be moved with compassion and still pray with authority.

Free to shudder with fear or pain and not be dominated by either . . . and pray again.

And free to fight.

To invade.

The impossible yields before prayer.

And there is room for those who will seek to learn how all prayer makes all things possible.

15.
THE MOST PRAYED
PRAYER IN THE WORLD

There is a majesty to these words that Jesus taught His disciples to pray. Somehow, when they are transmitted in song over the airwaves, peace fills millions of hearts. When they are employed liturgically, their cadence seems to quiet our souls, and the content seems to move us to another place—to a better time.

A man is standing on a hillside. He's teaching. And in response to the request that He help His learners know how to pray, He pauses . . . then begins . . . when you pray, pray in this manner:

> Our Father,
>> Which art in heaven,
>> Hallowed be thy name.
> Thy kingdom come.
> Thy will be done
>> in earth, as it is in heaven.
> Give us this day our daily bread.
> And forgive us our debts,
>> as we forgive our debtors.

And lead us not into temptation,
  but deliver us from evil:
For thine is the kingdom,
  And the power,
  And the glory, for ever.
    Amen.

It's the most prayed prayer in the world: the Lord's Prayer, we call it. Some challenge that designation, saying, "It's the disciples' prayer—He gave it to them, told them to pray it." But He is the one who taught it. He is the one who breathed its depth of insight. He is the one who answered the request, "Teach us to pray." And He is the Lord.

And it is inconceivable—actually impossible—to deal with the meaning, the method, the power or the purposes of prayer without coming to it. And so we do.

Many who pray these words don't comprehend what they are saying, but that does not invalidate their speaking the prayer. God is wonderfully patient with us. We can be thankful that His principal way of evaluating us is by looking on our hearts. If His appraisals were based on what He found in our minds—either their interests, their information or their ignorances—we would all be miserably set by.

But who knows?

There is every reason to believe that each time that prayer is spoken from the heart, irrespective of how little the worshiper may understand of what he says, that God takes the requested action.

For the eyes of the Lord run to and fro throughout the whole earth, to shew himself strong in the behalf of them whose heart is perfect toward him . . . (II Chronicles 16:9).

However, it is our desire to deepen our grasp of this great prayer, so we will examine the principles Jesus was emphasizing in it.

Our first quotation of it was from Matthew 6:9-13. For this outline we will use its other appearance in the Gospels, Luke 11:2-4. It lacks the concluding ascription—"for thine is the kingdom," etc.—which I have added from Matthew. Otherwise, though, some of its less familiar phrases may help us think more deeply on its meaning. Open your Bible there (to Matthew) and compare with Luke's record here as we study.

Theme	Truth	Taught
Worship	All prayer is to begin with appropriate praise and adoration of the Father.	Our Father which art in heaven, Hallowed be thy name.
Rulership	All prayer should somehow invite His will to work earthward.	Thy kingdom come. Thy will be done, as in heaven, so in earth.
Provision	God is concerned for daily detail, and we should ask about it.	Give us day by day our daily bread.
Forgiveness	We should not approach God without acknowledging our need for cleansing.	And forgive us our sins . . .
Release	Nor can we overlook God's outlook on relationships.	. . .for we also forgive every one that is indebted to us.
Progress	And we must set our wills to mature.	And lead us not into temptation; but deliver us from evil.
Surrender	All prayer concludes by placing everything in God's hands.	For thine is the kingdom, and the power, and the glory, for ever. Amen.

It is marvelously complete. No point of experience or issue in life is not included. An exposition of the abundance of meaning in these words would fill volumes.

Our commentary will be brief, but the principles are worthy of pursuit by each one who would desire a lifetime of growth in prayer.

First: All prayer is to begin with appropriate praise and adoration of the Father: "Our Father which art in heaven, hallowed be thy name."

Two factors are involved in this principle: The direction *of* prayer and our attitude *in* prayer.

"When you pray say, 'Our Father.' " With these two words the Lord Jesus was stressing the nature of the Almighty One. We are not approaching a cold-hearted deity or an unpredictable super human. What Jesus wanted us to grasp in speaking these words is often limited by the relationship we have known with an earthly parent. But God cannot be mirrored in the image of any human being except His Son. "The only begotten Son, who has come from the Father's own heart, He has expressly declared His nature and being" (John 1:18, paraphrase).

We are coming to a living God, and a loving God. He *is*. And He *loves you!*

The words "Our Father" also give us the precise point of address in our prayers. This is not a complex matter, but it is worthy of discernment. Our asking—petitions, requests, desires for divine intervention—is to be addressed to the Father. This is what Jesus was saying in His upper room discourse, only hours before His arrest and death on the cross, when He said: "At that day you will not ask me for anything. But indeed, I assure you that whatever you ask the Father in my name, he will give it to you" (John 16:23).

Considerable issue has been made of this point by purists who insist that we are not to pray to Jesus. A certain residue of doubt or condemnation has fallen out from such legalistic blasts. But there is an actual truth to be learned.

No member of the Godhead is jealous of the other, for the mystery of the Trinity—so insoluble to finite minds—is perfectly comprehensible and compatibly experienced by the Father, Son and Holy Spirit. But there is an intended order of approach in prayer. Without becoming unduly technical, let us realize that:

The Father is the one addressed with requests. His will and way are sought, and His Word is the promise we take in believing we shall be heard.

Jesus, the Son, is the one in whose name we come. His saving, redeeming life-gift includes the privilege of entering the throne room of heaven.

The Holy Spirit assists us in our praying. He has been poured out upon us as a personalized communicator of the Father's love, and He helps us exalt and magnify the Lord Jesus Christ.

The Trinity is to be worshiped: "Praise Father, Son and Holy Ghost," the doxology lauds.

The Father is to be petitioned.

The Son is to be glorified.

The Holy Spirit is to be honored.

Petitioning the Father acknowledges His right to rule and decide in all matters.

Glorifying Jesus the Savior is exalting Him who died that we might live.

Honoring the Holy Spirit is giving place to His workings in and through our lives.

Then we come to the matter of our attitude in prayer.

Far too frequently the mere mention of the Trinity prompts a puzzled squint of the eyes instead of a humbled bowing of the heart. But a clearheaded "Our Father" will bring forth a full-hearted "hallowed be Thy name," *Holy* be your name is the meaning. This is Christ's instruction to worship the Father after the same manner as those marvelous beings around His eternal throne who rest not day and night, saying, "Holy, holy, holy, Lord God Almighty, which was, and is, and is to come" (Revelation 4:8). Since the meaning of holiness is essentially completeness, the worship of the Father as "Holy, Holy, Holy," is not an unoriginal mouthing of religious verbiage. It is the acknowledgment of His nature—His changelessness, His dependability, His total integrity.

This opening of "the most prayed prayer" lifts prayer far beyond the finest the flesh can utter. It is being borne upward by the Holy Spirit and attended to by the Father. And He will always respond to those who worship (1) in spirit and, (2) in truth (John 4:23).

The Holy Spirit provides the former.

Jesus' instruction on how to begin provides the latter.

Second: All prayer should somehow invite His will to work earthward: "Thy kingdom come. Thy will be done, as in heaven, so in earth."

The God we worship is the Lord of creation, and His power knows no limits except those He imposes on Himself. Here is one of them. He waits to work His will on earth in answer to humans who ask. His kingdom—His eternal rulership—will only rule on earth where it is invited. It is not a question of His ability to dominate on the sheer strength of His own intent, but it is the fact that with reference to earth and man He has chosen to confine himself to specific channels of operation. He wills to work through people. Rebels may resist, sin may abound, but He will find someone through whom to work.

100

Jesus is saying, "Let it be you."

Isaiah records, "And he saw that there was no man, and wondered that there was no intercessor: therefore his arm brought salvation unto him; and his righteousness, it sustained him" (59:16). His following verses prophesy the coming of the Redeemer, and make clear that, when sin's impact rendered it impossible for God to find a man through whom to work, He became one himself.

The incarnation shows that God has willed to work all redemptive operations through man; and the establishment of the church (far different than the church as an establishment) is the evidence that both the Father and the Son want that process to flow now through its agency. God works redemption through the church (Ephesians 3:10), which is people who call upon His rule to invade the mischievous and merciless works of satanic powers. It is by this kind of praying—that opposes hellish operations in heaven's name—that He receives "glory in the church by Christ Jesus" (Ephesians 3:21).

Jesus says, when you pray, and after you have come before the Father with worship, begin to call for His will to be worked on earth. That's the only way it's going to happen here—when those who want His will to be done declare that it be. It is through these redeemed men and women that God remains faithful to His self-imposed limits—only to work on earth through mankind—and still is able to cast out evil in all its manifestations.

Third: God is concerned for daily detail, and we should ask about it: "Give us day by day our daily bread."

The most important thing about this is not the discovery that we can ask for God's help in the mundane matters of our personal lives. The most important thing is that we are told to. The message is plain. We must ask about day-to-day matters as

101

well as large eternal issues. Back-to-back with prayer that the Almighty's will be worked on earth, we should not overlook the simplest matters of life.

This doesn't mean we should worry about them. Quite the opposite. "Your heavenly Father knows that you need such things. . . . Take therefore no thought . . ." (Matthew 6:32, 34). But it does mean not to neglect asking Him to be your provider.

By God's grace we come to realize that the work of our own hands provides *nothing*. Not that God has appointed us to laziness, but "God helps those who help themselves" *isn't* in the Bible. "Ask for your day by day need" is. And full understanding in prayer leads us to consult the Father about the smallest matters in life . . . which, in fact, inevitably become the largest if neglected in prayer.

Fourth: We should not approach God without acknowledging our need for cleansing: "And forgive us our sins. . . ."

Somehow it is difficult to register this point without conveying the idea that Jesus was seeking to "keep those sinners in place!" The directive to regularly confess sin could be, to the mind of the misguided, a prompting to sustain a sense of guilt or condemnation.

But, of course, we know Jesus better than that.

He's not a condemner. "For God sent not his Son into the world to condemn the world; but that the world through him might be saved" (John 3:17). Nonetheless, He said that the way to pray includes confession of sin. He was gently but pointedly underscoring the fact that (1) the Father cannot take note of prayer from a petitioner who is more interested in getting than in godliness; and that (2) the Father will forgive those who ask.

It's not a "beg and hope" proposition.

Christ wouldn't have taught this prayer priority if the Father wasn't disposed to receive sinners. Like the father of the prodigal child who came with open acknowledgment of his failure, the heavenly Father waits for our request for forgiveness and then delights to use that occasion to spread a feast of His goodness before us (Luke 15:21-23).

This is a continual need: "If we say that we have no sin, we deceive ourselves and the truth is not in us" (I John 1:8).

And there is a continual answer: "If we confess our sins, he is faithful and just to forgive us our sins, and to cleanse us from all unrighteousness" (I John 1:9).

Fifth: Nor can we overlook God's outlook on relationships: ". . . for we also forgive every one that is indebted to us."

Jesus prohibits a vertical approach to God that neglects a horizontal approach to people. His insistence—indeed, the Godhead's order of things—is established in words that astonish us with a hard spiritual fact: our being forgiven is contingent upon our forgiving-ness. Our answers *from* Him depend upon our wills to answer *unto* Him.

God refuses to raise a breed of sons and daughters who are unlike Him. He has sired us. He insists that every latent trait of our former heritage, as offspring of Adam's race, be wormed out of us. He won't allow unforgiveness to continue. It's not in His nature, so He confronts it in ours.

Jesus' teaching could produce prayer something like this:

Father, I ask you to forgive me for today's particular failings and points of disobedience, and . . . oh, by the way, Lord: I must confess the irritation that sprang up today when Pat and I crossed each other. Even now, your Holy Spirit is prodding me to acknowledge that a seed of bitterness was blown into my mind by that encounter.

Lord, I refuse to allow that seed to take root.

I ask you to help me to be truly understanding of Pat. Whether the action was intentional or accidental, I refuse to attempt becoming judge of the matter. You are the judge of hearts, and I place mine before you for your working, Father.

As the first work, forgive me;
> for even now I forgive Pat . . .
>> from my heart.

I do forgive and release this person from all cravings and clutchings of my flesh to exact some toll for having offended me. I am indebted to you, Father, for your constant forgiveness. Remembering that, I will not—I cannot—charge another for any offense against me. Thank you for helping me, Father, through the power of the blood of Jesus and the grace you have released through His cross. *Amen.*

That's maturity in motion. And it's the way to pray . . . and to insure prayers are answered. The altar of the Almighty must be approached in accord with His principles. That is the spirit of Jesus' words 'n Matthew 5:23,24.

Therefore if hou bring thy gift to the altar, and there rememberest that thy brother hath ought against thee; Leave there thy gift before the altar, and go thy way; first be reconciled to thy brother, and then come and offer thy gift.

Relationship takes precedence over worship. That's shocking to our "spiritual" presuppositions, isn't it? But it's the Word of God from the lips of His Son. And it cannot be disregarded without paying the price of disobedience in prayer.

How peculiar can disobedience be! Me? Disobey while I pray?

Yes. That's the message.

If I don't permit the forgiveness I have received to flow on to the forgiving of others, I hinder true and fulfilling relationships with those I bind up to the debt I feel they owe me.

God won't allow it.

And the penalty for violating this principle is more than merely not having my prayers answered. I find myself bound up in chains forged by my own unforgiveness. It's a plague to the flesh, grudge-bearing is. But my release of others is the pathway to deliverance from it.

Don't forget it.

You can't be unforgiving.

And when you're hurt by another. Forget it.

After you forgive it.

Sixth: And we must set our wills to mature: "And lead us not into temptation; but deliver us from evil."

This is a tough text because James 1:13 says, "God tempts no one, nor can He be tempted with sin." So, why do we need to pray that He won't do what He never does? It seems as though the Savior is saying, "You should pray regularly that God won't trick you into some trap He has for you," or, "If you ask, God might be nice enough not to throw you to Satan's wolves." But that is not the case.

Nor is it a plea for His kindness not to arrange tests that are more than we can bear. I Corinthians 10:13 magnificently takes care of that.

There is no test, trial or temptation that will come upon you but that many have passed that way before. God knows what you face, and He will faithfully see that it never exceeds what you can survive. In fact, you can be sure He will make a way of escape so that you can flee free of it (paraphrase).

What we have here is a special facet of prayer which Jesus taught; one which cannot be understood apart from linking it with the last part of the sentence. The two work in tandem: "Don't bring us in, but bring us out!"

The spirit of the text argues that we understand the Lord's instruction as a summons to maturity. He is saying, "When you pray, acknowledge that the Father isn't your problem when temptation assails you, but that He is your protector."

The pray-er who is willing to grow up as the Father's son or daughter is one who is learning to tell the difference between the refining tests which purge and purify (I Peter 1:6, 7; 4:12, 13) and the destructive assaults of Satan (Luke 22:31) or of the base cravings of the flesh (James 1:14-16). His prayer, in effect, is saying: "Father, I believe you won't lead me into temptation . . . but I also call upon you to deliver me from the evil one." (The evil one, personalized, is a possible translation of this portion of the verse.)

The pray-er who is willing to mature is also one who is available to specific instances of God's delivering grace in his life. Only the most superficial analyses of God's salvation process deny this need. "Who delivered us from so great a death, who doth deliver; in whom we trust that he will yet deliver us" (II Corinthians 1:10). Here is the sanctifying process of God's deliverance at work in our lives: past, present and future. The kind of person the Lord Jesus is describing here prays, "I know there's room to grow, Father. I also find from time to time that there is a stranglehold on part of my life; habits or thought patterns or unrighteous residue of my past. But as I pray, I am affirming my desire that you perfect me—constantly enlarging the borders of my inheritance by delivering me from whatever would halt or hinder my becoming like your Son. Evict everything that encroaches. Mature me in your image, in Jesus' Name."

Finally: All prayer concludes by placing everything in God's hands: "For thine is the kingdom, and the power, and the glory, for ever. *Amen.*"

Surrender—best demonstrated by that posture which lifts both hands and waits in helplessness inviting mercy—is the ultimate act of prayer. Quite honestly, there's little else to do after all.

Prayer may be filled with faith, uttered with boldness, offered in obedience and overflowing with praise and confidence. But after all is said, it's still up to Him.

What I am about to say might be misinterpreted, but it must be asserted: This surrender declares that we need to learn a position that will prevail whatever happens. He isn't saying, "Brace for a failure by casting yourself in a grand act of surrender." But He is teaching us this: "Your best finale is the declaration of His unchallengeable majesty. After you've worshiped and petitioned to the best of your Holy-Spirit-energized ability, rest it all with Him. The answers may not come in the size packages you suppose, or be delivered at the moment you have in mind. But trust Him. All power and glory are His. And in freely and praisefully speaking that, you open the door to His invitation that you share it with Him . . . in His way, at His time."

16.
THE PRAYING THAT ENLARGES MILLIONS

This chapter is about speaking with tongues or, more precisely, praying to God or praising the Lord by means of a language one has not learned.

Division.

That's the word that always comes up. Say "tongues," and the next word you will hear from many quarters will be "division."

And there *is* division on the subject. Indictments seem to fly like snowflakes on a blustery winter night in Maine—

"Hank and Edna were such faithful members until they got into this 'charismatic' thing."

"Charlie, I don't care if you do it in private, but, please, don't speak about 'tongues' in your Sunday school class."

"The decision of the Board of Trustees is herewith announced, that anyone who believes in or exercises the experience of glossolalia or 'speaking with tongues' shall be outside the doctrine of this church, and therefore should remove himself from fellowship."

And the snowdrifts. In fact, an entire snowbank has risen

between people, all of who love Jesus in solid, biblical faith. Division exists, but it is foolish to try to say who is responsible for it. One thing is clear, from whichever side you attempt to reach the other, you inevitably feel the chill. It's hard to burrow through a snowdrift and even harder to see through one.

Ask a partisan from either side why the great divide—like snow covered Rockies—exists, and the "snow job" increases.

Pro:	Con:
They kicked me out.	Their attitude became intolerable.
I tried to show love, but I was regarded somehow as "leprous."	They claimed to be "loving" but they clearly felt superior to all of us.
The Bible says, "Forbid not to speak with tongues." They did.	We believe the Bible. It gives clear teaching against exaggerated emphasis on tongues.

And that's only a smattering of the kind of exchange between those who insist and those who resist. In fact, they would apply those two verbs to one another. Each would claim to be properly insistent on the truth of the Word of God, and each would be inclined to say the other resists some spiritual value. It would require an entire book to even begin to deal with the various shades of opinion and practice that characterize the two camps.

But our purpose is not to examine the "tongues question." Our purpose is *prayer*. We must honestly deal with as many aspects of prayer as we discover in the Scriptures. And speaking with tongues is a means of prayer.

"He that speaks in a tongue is not speaking to men but unto God" (I Corinthians 14:2). "For if I pray in a tongue, my spirit is praying" (I Corinthians 14:14). "What shall I do then? I will pray with the spirit and I will pray with the understanding also" (I Corinthians 14:15).

We deal with glossolalia only to increase dimensions of prayer. Let us call it "spiritual language," since speaking with tongues is an enablement of the Holy Spirit exercised by the human spirit (my spirit is praying). Prayer in a language we understand is not unspiritual or less spiritual than praying in tongues. Neither kind of prayer is inherently superior to the other, but, like different breeds of horses, has different uses.

Spiritual language primarily aids prayer. Why else would Paul have so boldly thanked God for it? Why else would he have thanked God that he spoke in tongues more than all of his readers (I Corinthians 14:18)?

He wasn't attempting to make a doctrinal point on "the sign" of an initial experience in the Holy Spirit. Instead, he was speaking about a continual practice.

Nor was he talking about acquired linguistic skills for world evangelism. Otherwise in the following verse he would not speak of his preference to "speak five words that can be understood" when in a public meeting.

He didn't say it to encourage fanatical display or pointless babblings. To the contrary, in the context he told them to stop such nonsense.

And he certainly wasn't taking sides in some controversy between the "tongues speakers" and the "non-tongues speakers." The purpose of his whole letter is to bridge divisions and implant love.

The apostle is declaring something excellent in his experience. The Holy Spirit prompted Paul to speak about a practice over which there was no *contention* in the New

Testament church at large, but over which there was *confusion* in the Corinthian congregation. Why was this subject important enough to spend as much time and space on it as the Scriptures do; and valuable enough to elicit such high commentary from the apostle?

It is because he links tongues to prayer and praise. He states, "I will with the spirit" (v. 15) and, he adds, in doing so, one "gives thanks well" (v. 17).

The manner in which the theme is treated indicates that in Corinth spiritual language was accepted, approved, valued and not to be discouraged. Thus, "speaking with tongues" was established as worthwhile. Today it would be good to see spiritual language deemed worthwhile again—worthy to employ in prayer.

So we are bothering to deal with this controversial topic which irritates many sincere believers. But it's worth the risk of opening wounds in those who have been offended by ignorant and totally unnecessary abuses or exaggerated emphases. It's also worth the risk that others, whose exaggerations or fanaticism plague the tastes of the sensitive, may consider inclusion of the subject as a "victory" for their side.

Prayer is the reason, prayer that will invade the impossible with effective, Holy Spirit energy. Prayer which penetrates the impenetrable by transcending the perceptible.

Our quest may produce understanding which will help melt the snowbank. Without probing the questions of (1) the relationship of spiritual language to Holy Spirit baptism, or (2) the exercise of the gift of tongues in the midst of the congregation, let us deal with spiritual language for the purposes of prayer.

Conceivably, this will bring us to the crucial point of realizing the deepest purpose of this gift. Isn't it possible that the expanded communication which the spiritual language affords is the underlying and real reason for the conflict raised on the subject? Isn't it possible that the opponents are not nearly as animated by a selfish insistence on their own views as by a satanic manipulation that hinders all of our views?

Might it be that the smoke of hellfire has wafted into the camp of the faithful, and caused tears of blindness to block our view? And, worse, in our blindness do we fail to recognize the real source of the smoke?

If the adversary can pit his opponents against one another over a practice which is potentially destructive to his operations, and cause believers to accuse each other of being blinded by him (while in fact both are smarting from his smoke in their eyes, and thinking that they themselves are the only side seeing clearly), then how great would be the frustration to the Holy Spirit's design to enlarge our prayer?

Spiritual language has been given, beyond any other reason, to expand communication in prayer.

To describe it as solely for that purpose would be unscriptural, but it is essentially for prayer. This is certainly why "speaking to God" is the first use mentioned in I Corinthians 14. When Paul relates the revelation of God's correct and intended employment of spiritual language, he mentions prayer first. Other beneficial uses may be studied with profit, for all God's gifts are worthy of our understanding. But primary in our view is the place of the spiritual language in prayer.

"Still, why?"

First, let's consider the benefits of the spiritual language as supra-intellectual praying.

By *supra* we are describing prayer that is beyond the mind. Notice:

(1) It is not *infra*, beneath the intellect. That is, this is not incoherent speech. Incoherent suggests the person

doesn't know what he is doing or saying. In the exercise of spiritual language, the believer knows both. What he is doing is speaking in other tongues, exercising the privilege on his own volition. He is not in a trance, a seizure or a state of ecstasy, as so many misinformed descriptions would suggest. Further, what he is saying are words that are motivated by the Holy Spirit, addressed to the Father, and approved of the Lord Jesus (Mark 16:17).

(2) And it is not *contra*, against the intellect. Speaking with tongues is neither an overwhelming nor an anti-intellectual experience. This mistaken idea stems from the joyful exuberance that sometimes attends a person's first entry into this experience. Personal testimonies which describe the first exercise of spiritual language often exude an enthusiasm which thwarts objective understanding by the hearer. But these same testimonies tend to establish the criteria for "speaking with tongues." They make it sound like a "Holy Ghost high"—a transcendental trip of some type.

But prayer in the spiritual language is neither wild nor weird. On the contrary, it is sane, practical exercise which is only as emotional as the temperament of the one exercising the gift. I am not disannulling my mind or dismantling my perspective on good sense. I am speaking to God in a way God makes available to those who ask.

Human intellects are finite.

Few would disagree with that statement. We laugh, "I sure don't claim to know everything!" But a subtle irony is present even in that answer. We think we know how much we don't know. We agree outwardly, but inwardly we hate to be told anything. Knowledge is power. Knowledge exalts. Ignorance demeans.

One wonders how great a breakthrough is needed for us to acknowledge how little we actually do know, and of the little we know, how very little we really understand, and of the little we understand, how inadequate our ability to express it, and with what ability we have, how seldom we really exercise it.

The Apostle Paul undoubtedly made the breakthrough and, though he is perhaps the most intellectual writer in the New Testament, had a pretty accurate appraisal of the serious limitations of his active mind. That is one reason, I think, why he was thankful that he could speak in tongues. The burden of the churches was great upon him and, consequently, his need to pray was enormous. More than likely he often resorted to his spiritual language, especially when he felt the desire to pray but was not sure why or even for whom.

Those who have employed this practice for years will tell you that it has given them a new breadth of continuity in prayer. During the course of the day, a subject for prayer will come to mind, and the spiritual language employed in an almost silent utterance. While the precise content of the prayer is not known, the subject is. Work or travel are hardly interrupted. Intercessions or supplications with the spirit *and* with the understanding are possible. The mind initiates the exercise, but is freed from the responsibility to supply words and ideas.

The "unutterable groans" or "deep sighings" in Romans 8:26 come to mind when we discuss praying with the spiritual language. It certainly provides a capacity to pray when "we don't know how to pray as we should." And, best of all, such prayer is "according to the will of God." I don't know what to pray, and, therefore, how to pray, but the Holy Spirit makes it possible for me to pray, and to do it exactly in line with God's eternal and sovereign purposes.

In Ephesians 6:18, "Praying with all prayer and supplication in the spirit" must be—indeed cannot be otherwise —recognized as referring to spiritual language, for essentially the same terminology is utilized in I Corinthians 14:14-16. There we read, "If I pray in a tongue, my spirit is praying. . . . So then, I will pray with the spirit." We cannot tell whether the word "spirit" should be capitalized or not in either passage. But whether it refers to my spirit or the Holy Spirit, "praying with the spirit" involves speaking in tongues.

Spiritual language in prayer is *not* the same as the public gift of tongues. That very point of confusion afflicted the Corinthian worship gatherings. The people made no distinction between the exercising of their spiritual language (intended for use in private prayer) and the public exercise of the gift of tongues (which was *always* to be interpreted for the benefit of the other worshipers). This, by the way, explains an apparent contradiction between I Corinthians 12:30—"Do all speak with tongues?" (in context Paul obviously expects a "no" answer—not all speak with tongues) and I Corinthians 14:5—"I wish that you all spoke with tongues." The former passage refers to tongues in public worship, the latter to tongues in private prayer.

Any believer may enjoy the benefit of spiritual language in prayer. Jesus said that those who believe in Him will speak with new tongues (Mark 16:17).

The Holy Spirit controls the distribution of the gifts—including the choice as to when He wishes to prompt, for example, "a tongue" (with the completing gift of its "interpretation"). In the matter of prayer, however, He gives to all who ask another tongue in which to pray. There is no reason to doubt or fear. And there is every reason to ask, for we need all the ability to pray we can receive.

Asking is the prerequisite for receiving. Yet hosts of believers have never asked for the benefit of a spiritual language for prayer. People haven't asked for this because:

1. They didn't know the possibility existed.
2. They have been told it is unscriptural.
3. They have seen fanatical displays.
4. They have heard bizarre stories.
5. They think "tongues" is a seizure.
6. They have been told it is outdated.
7. They have been afraid it is only emotionalism.

But fresh air can blow away the smoke screen if we will open the windows to the breeze of the Spirit. "If ye then, being evil, know how to give good gifts unto your children, how much more shall your Father which is in heaven give good things to them that ask him?" (Matthew 7:11). "For the Lord God is a sun and shield: the Lord will give grace and glory: no good thing will he withhold from them that walk uprightly" (Psalm 84:11).

While we are *not* saying to ask for the "gift of tongues," for we have made the distinction earlier between the public gift (Greek, *charisma*) and the private one (Greek, *dorea*), it would be appropriate to add an explanation for any who may feel this distinction is artificial.

We are not suggesting the wholesale entry into the courtroom of heaven to demand that we be given "the gift of tongues." Nor are we asking anyone to change their doctrinal opinions about the baptism with the Holy Spirit.

But we are suggesting that you and I can be pray-ers with a broader spectrum of coverage, an often greater accuracy in requests, and greater effectiveness as an intercessor or supplicator.

Let's allow the Holy Spirit to fulfill His wish in us—His wish that "you all speak with tongues." The pathway to that privilege is in humble, praiseful worship before the Lord Jesus Christ. Perhaps the prayer that follows will prove helpful.

Lord Jesus, I come to you, without presumption, to ask for

an enlarged capacity in prayer. Because you have made me worthy through your blood, I will not fear to ask freely. I trust you, dear Lord, never to give me an injurious gift. Overflow my lips with new expressions of praise to the Father, prayers in thy name, all by the power of the Holy Spirit. *Amen.*

17.
THE PRAYING THAT
SETS BOUNDARIES

There is a basic sense of proportion in most everyone that tells them when things "don't fit" or when something "doesn't belong." It's primarily an aesthetic sense that sees how things contribute to or violate beauty. While tastes vary greatly and relativism has taught many to demonstrate their "broadmindedness" by insisting there is a beauty even in ugliness, a basic sense of proportion still resides in the hearts of those who require simple honesty of themselves.

We can tell when that which is alien is present. It doesn't take a great deal of discernment to pick out the object which is not color coordinated with its room, to recognize the musical note which is discordant with the melody line in progress, or to identify the accessory that clashes with the style of an outfit of clothes.

Most people—if they're simply candid about it and skip the philosophizing—can spot that which intrudes. Something in us signals the violation of boundaries. Unless one's values are jaded by ceaseless compromise or the conscience seared by rationalized wickedness, the human spirit cries, "Foul!"

119

We read a novel or see a show in which an interloper, through subtle manipulations, gradually overcomes his victim. We are aware of his sinister encroaching upon boundaries of what is not properly his. His encroachment eventually becomes domination. Like a snake silently stalking its sleeping prey, slowly coiling about it, finally engulfing it and smothering the victim behind jaws that open into a destiny of darkness and death, the operations of evil swallow the attempts of men to live fulfilled lives.

And that's the scene.

The cast of characters:

Snake/Interloper: Satan, your adversary the devil.

Prey/Victim: Interchangeably, you, me, the neighbor next door, the child down the street who died of leukemia, the businessman who surrendered to financial pressure and absconded with funds, the clergyman who was lured by sexual temptation and fell, the politician who succumbed to repeated offers, the family ties that slowly dissolved by imperceptible steps of decay until "one day we fell apart" . . . and the show goes on.

The location:

Our planet. Intended for blessing, it fell under the accursed rule of the serpent. However, this scenario indicates most scenes are to be shot in the invisible realm, which most men deny or seldom sense. What is shot is irresistibly played back in the visible realm where humans experience the horrors of what hell has previously scripted for them.

The plot:

Filled with conflict and violence, it unfolds the actions of two forces—righteousness and unrighteousness—under the leadership of two personalities—Christ and Satan. The conflict's ultimate resolution has already been determined in a strange but decisive battle actually won by the righteous one through His death on the cross. But the conflict is still in progress. The author, in the meantime, has also scripted roles for each creature. He has outlined a purpose for each of them—consistent with His likeness and nature. The interloper, Satan, presses his encroaching designs upon them. He only succeeds in the measure that he is allowed by the creatures, since all that is permitted to occur in this setting is up to them.

The dialogue:
The adversary's role involves a succession of tirades against the creator, boastings against the Almighty, coupled with his lying whispers to the creatures he relentlessly afflicts. He consistently blames God for all suffering, or he indicts the sufferer with a stream of accusations designed to deepen his distress, from guilt to condemnation, or from despair to futility, or from self-pity to suicide, or from rancor to rooted bitterness.

The answer to the adversary's allegations is upon the tongues of those who follow the righteous one. But somehow, because the drama takes place in the invisible realm first, most of the spokesmen for righteousness seem confused. They tend to deal with symptoms rather than causes; with the problem rather than its source. They often bog down in past muttered irritation, frustrated complaint or mystified inquiry. But even when they actually move into prayer (the only instrument that can function in this conflict), they seldom hit the mark. They more often pray desperately about the adversary's workings than they join together to declare his destruction. The fundamental problem: The victims seem unaware of the tactics of the interloper, and, even when they do, they are generally too slow to deploy weapons which could intersect his operations.

And therein hangs the tale.

But not its end, because the conclusion is yet to be written by those who learn to shape events through prayer. Human history, once penetrated by the Lord of life, is subjected to rewrite even now. But the launching of such a project requires (1) the abandonment of a fatalistic attitude toward trying circumstances, and (2) the commitment of those who know Him to learn His ways of triumph.

To accomplish the first requirement we assert God's beneficent nature and affirm that all that robs life of joy is not His will. To accomplish the second requires instruction in a major tactic of prayer: intercession—the praying that sets boundaries.

First, we must discard an idea about intercession that hinders many of us. The stories of such great men of prayer as George Mueller, David Brainerd, Rees Howells and "Praying" Hyde have a peculiar effect on us. As thrilling as these testimonies are, they tend to intimidate us. This doesn't mean there's anything wrong with their lives. The problem lies instead with us in our unbelief. The sweeping majority of believers do not believe they could rise to effective intercession. But you and I must turn around and decide that powerful praying is our potential as well. And that it isn't at the remote end of some impassable jungle trail.

Intercession can be a part of our lives now—the kind of prayer that invades the impossible and sets *new* boundaries of possibility.

Now we are ready to begin the quest for discovery. Open a Bible to examine several verses we will be discussing.

To begin with, we ought to look at the Greek word, *entunchano* (verb), *enteuxis* (noun). One or the other occurs in the principal passages on intercession: Romans 8:26, 27, 34; I Timothy 2:1 and Hebrews 7:25. The paucity of the occurrence of these words in the New Testament should not reduce their importance to us. Intercession is strategic in the three areas which redemption primarily affects:

1. The relationship of the individual with God (Hebrews 7:25; Romans 8:34).

2. The working of the Holy Spirit in the individual (Romans 8:26, 27).

3. The influence of the whole church on the social order (I Timothy 2:1-4).

These texts show that intercession directly affects what happens between involved parties. The parties may be God and man, man and man, or men and nations, but intercession has shaping influence in all three realms. It is more than asking, it is a controlling influence on possibilities.

The basic idea of *entunchano* is "to make an appeal." From that it has taken on broader implications. Lexicons show the root idea of this word to be, "to light upon by chance, to meet accidentally." So it expresses a fortuitous and unplanned encounter of parties. That definition seems pointless unless we take into consideration God's stratagems for prayer. Let's further build our understanding with a passage, part of which we considered briefly in a preceding chapter: Romans 8:26, 27.

Even so, the Spirit helps us in our weakness. We do not know what to pray for, if we are to pray as we ought, but the Spirit himself intercedes for us, when the only prayers that we can offer are inarticulate cries. He who penetrates into the inmost depths of the human heart knows what the Spirit means, for it is by God's will that the Spirit pleads for God's people (Barclay).

Once in each of these two verses in Romans the word *entunchano*, intercession, occurs. "We don't know how to pray as we ought," the Scripture says, "so the Holy Spirit helps our weakness by making intercessions." The Third Person of the Godhead is active in (1) bringing to mind people or circumstances we ought to pray for, and (2) giving rise to prayer

123

that exactly hits the mark. That is, God himself knows where hearts cry for His intervention, and the Holy Spirit prompts prayer to release the working of His hand for them.

This is a distinct enablement of the Holy Spirit in prayer, but it is also prayer in the context of situations which are either too complex or remote for our complete understanding, or ones in which our deepest emotions are stirred with an aching sense of out-of-joint-ness.

The preceding verses, Romans 8:19-25, describe the whole universe as experiencing trauma, groaning for God's ultimate concluding of His redemptive plan. All creation is aware that an offender has transgressed the universal order of things. From throughout the galaxies a cry—doubtless angelic in its origin—for reestablished order is coming forth. Angels sang praise to the eternal Father at creation (Job 38:4-7); now they express their yearning plea for the expulsion of the encroacher. They are groaning for a restoration of the boundaries of righteousness throughout the heavens.

And then, another groaning is mentioned—ours. Each after its own order. Creation's groaning is celestial, ours is terrestrial. Creation longs for the ultimate consummation of God's purposes, we for an immediate development within those purposes. Creation's time is future. Our time is now. The Holy Spirit is teaching us to pray for the expulsion of all that offends the Almighty's purpose here—on earth.

Earlier in this chapter we used some terms to help establish a perspective on intercession. Now compare these columns:

that which is alien—boundaries
that which intrudes—sense what doesn't belong
encroachment—resist
interloper—intersect, cut off

We see in them a climate of conflict, an effort to ward off an offending poacher, an insistence that the "squatter" has no rights. Compare that with the groan this text relates.

This is the spirit of intercession, a bold withstanding through prayer of whatever asserts itself against God's benevolent designs for mankind. It is staggering to even begin to realize that the whole process by which God's will is done on earth depends on an interceding church. Just as groans of travail precede birth, so Holy-Spirit-begotten intercessions forecast new life, new hope and new possibilities for individuals trapped in the impossible.

God is always consistent with His own regulations. By sheer right of His sovereignty He could do anything, anywhere, at any time, by any means. But He doesn't. He confines himself to the redemptive processes worked through the cross of His Son and released by the ministry of the Holy Spirit through the church His Son redeemed. He will do nothing outside those channels. That is not to say there is nothing else He could do; it is to say, though, that there is no other way He will.

Intercessions—promptings that may come at any time ("to light upon by chance") for anyone ("to meet accidentally")—are a vital aspect of God's operations to rescue mankind. They help establish certain boundaries of righteousness. Without such intercession, hell breaks in like a volcano splitting the earth's crust and spewing lava, hellworkings overflow the surface of the earth. Intercession can cork the cone.

When I learn what intercession is, and how to respond to the Holy Spirit's prodding to do it, I am moving into partnership with the Father in the highest sense (John 17:21, 23; Romans 8:14-17; Galatians 4:1-7).

Such understanding is valuable in terms of my ability to recognize the promptings, because I can know what to do when even a passing concern comes to mind regarding any person or thing. The very rise of concern is enough reason for intercession. I also know how to respond whenever I feel an urging in my heart toward prayer, but without knowing exactly for what or whom I should pray. With the aid of the Holy Spirit I can simply begin, saying, "Spirit of God, help me to pray. I sense your prompting me to intercede. I want to cooperate with you." Thus, if you pray with the spirit (I Corinthians 14:15), you will find that effective intercession is under way. What I'm saying is clearly stated in the lyrics of the old spiritual, "Every Time I Feel the Spirit Movin' in My Heart, I Pray."

Anything unwelcomed and unbidden may be resisted when it crowds in upon a circumstance. Noting the three main categories of life in which intercession potentially plays so great a part, I can act.

1. When I fail, I stumble, I hurt—and then I call on the Lord Jesus Christ. My call becomes His prompting, and He takes my situation to the Father.

> He is able to rescue entirely all those who come to God by the avenue of His priesthood, inasmuch as He is alive forevermore and thereby available to intercede for them (Hebrews 7:25, paraphrase).

2. When an individual or group is in a crisis, prayer is needed, but many who ought to pray don't know of the circumstance. Then the Holy Spirit prompts receptive believers to pray. He may indicate the subject, or He may simply move the respondents toward prayer.

> The Spirit takes hold of us in our weakness, for we don't know what to pray for; but He supercedes our inadequacy by bringing forth otherwise inarticulated intercessions. He knows what the will of God is, and He sees that these intercessions are according to His will in the interests of fellow believers (Romans 8:26,27, paraphrase).

3. A city, state or nation can be a believer's responsibility in prayer. There may or may not be a state of crisis or decay, but

whatever the case, the understanding pray-er assumes his intercessory role. The Word of God teaches that this kind of prayer superintendency is a primary appointment given the church by the Father ("I exhort that first of all . . .").

Prayers, intercessions and giving of thanks are a first line of responsibility you are to receive. Exercise this charge in behalf of all mankind, on behalf of political leaders and those holding responsibility for your society. It is by this means that you can experience a peaceful, quiet style of life in a godly and sensible way (I Timothy 2:1,2, paraphrase).

But we need to do more than recognize the basic meaning and significance of this prayer form. We should also realize its larger definition.

A few years ago the Holy Spirit began to lead the congregation which I pastor into an enlarged prayer responsibility. We felt we were supposed to pray (1) for people in calamitous situations; (2) for our country, which was undergoing a terrible political crisis; (3) for nations which were teetering on the brink of utter chaos, and (4) for the healing of physical afflictions—particularly those otherwise terminal in nature.

When that call came to us, I, the pastor, had little real understanding of the meaning and mechanics of intercession. All I could offer was a pat definition: "Intercession is praying in behalf of someone or thing." So I turned to the Bible and began my study in the New Testament, the fruits of which I have already shared in earlier pages. Then I turned my attention to the Old Testament. At first, I was puzzled that the first thirty-nine books of the Bible (KJV) only contained five references to intercession. I also found that the Hebrew verb *pagha'* (to intercede) had the same root meaning (to chance upon) as its Greek counterpart, *entunchano*. So that added nothing new. But I discovered that this one verb, *pagha'*, occurred in the Hebrew text forty-six times, although it was only translated to a form of the word "intercession" in five instances.

I was not troubled by this fact, for while I am not as familiar with Hebrew as with Greek, I was aware that Hebrew verbs take grammatical constructions that recommend varied translations.

But I was curious.

I began to look up each of the forty-six occurrences. Thirty-four of the forty-six references could be grouped into three concepts: thirteen times, the idea was "to fall upon"; thirteen times, the idea was "to light upon or to meet" (by chance); eight times, the idea was descriptive of borders "reaching unto" their assigned place.

Bible narratives in which the verb occurred produced examples of each grouping, and served to enlighten my own understanding of intercession. They show what happens when we respond to the Spirit's prompting to pray.

In Genesis 28:11, Jacob, who was running for his life from his twin brother Esau, "lighted upon a certain place, and tarried there all night, because the sun was set." The place was selected only because darkness had overtaken him there. Necessity alone governed his choice.

But at this "accidental" meeting place Jacob has the first of two life-transforming encounters with God himself. This place will be named Bethel (house of God), because Jacob, having met God there, will say, "Surely the LORD is in this place, and I knew it not" (v. 16). At that accidental meeting place Jacob received the revelation of God's purpose for his life. He was to inherit the land on which he was lying and, in the face of his present jeopardy, the future of his life was guaranteed.

There's a glimpse at what intercession is like—a place

"lighted upon" by accident.

When you are moved to pray for someone or something that comes to your mind "by accident," it is really God appointing and ordaining that meeting of the minds—His and ours—just as He selected the site of his encounter with Jacob. For whomever or whatever you pray, their destiny is shaped with certainty, and God's purpose realized through prayer. As the "lighting upon a certain place" ultimately affected Jacob, so our response to intercessory assignments which light upon our hearts may affect others. Intercession may guarantee someone a tomorrow because we obeyed the Holy Spirit today.

An especially striking example of *pagha'* is I Samuel 22:1-19. It is a tragic story, both in its outcome—eighty-five godly men were killed—and in the reason it happened.

Saul was jealously pursuing David and he believed, wrongly, that Ahimelech, the high priest, had betrayed him by granting assistance to David. When the king came upon Ahimelech he ordered his soldiers to kill the high priest and his attending aides. But none of his Hebrew troops would obey his command. (Saul's earlier unreasonable and unpredictable displays of rage had reduced the respect of his men.) And now, in view of the fact that to obey would mean to oppose the God of Israel, they were motionless before him.

Saul was rescued by a foreigner among his troops—Doeg. This man who, as an Edomite, had only contempt for the God of Israel, executed more than fourscore men. The Bible says "he fell upon [*pagha'*] the priests" (v. 18).

It's a terrible story to use as an illustration, but a truth is resident in it. Forget the horror. Forget the blight on Saul's spiritual life, forget the evil overflow of Doeg's heart, forget the blood-letting and the untimely deaths, forget the hideous example of a raging monarch mindlessly using his power for personal vindictiveness.

Then, remember that the use of this verb holds one meaningful truth: it is the readiness of a servant to do his master's will and attack his master's enemies on command. Prayer is an assault. There is a war to wage through prayer, and our king—the Lord Jesus Christ—is the commander of a host He seeks to teach to do battle in His name. But His is no personal vendetta, and ours is no cruel bloodshed.

The hearts of those who have done this sort of battle have felt the quickened pulse of prayers which are "falling upon" the adversary and his demonic hordes. Intercession is a principal instrument of spiritual warfare. "For the weapons of our warfare are not carnal, but mighty through God to the pulling down of strong holds" (II Corinthians 10:4). It is a means by which the Holy Spirit will cast down "every high thing that exalts itself against the knowledge of God" (v. 5).

The third way in which *pagha'* is used in the Bible best illustrates our chapter title, "The Praying That Sets Boundaries." In Joshua 19 *pagha'* is used six times (v. 11, 22, 26, 27 and twice in v. 34). It is tedious to read, because all that it contains is the designation of the border lines ordained for several tribes in Israel after the first stages of the conquest of Canaan. It is the sort of chapter one would skip easily, seeing little else in it besides an education in Bible geography.

But it's there and is translated "reaches to," designating that the boundaries given are intended to stretch all the way to prescribed points. They are not to be allowed to fall short, for that would diminish the intended possession of the tribe involved. In this setting *pagha'* speaks eloquently concerning intercessory principles.

The land was divided by lot, which meant that, by drawing straws or rolling dice, parcels of real estate were subdivided among the families of Israel. But it was not a gambling matter.

What appeared to be "chance" was, in the eyes of those who participated, a means by which they believed God manifested His will for each tribe. Proverbs 16:33 says, "The lot is cast into the lap; but the whole disposing thereof is of the Lord." A people's tribal boundaries were determined by God in what, for all human judgment, was only the turn of a card. He was in the midst of their "chance" operations, not because God supervises every role of the dice at the casinos of the world, but because they believed He thus would guide them.

We're dealing with the boundaries of God's inheritance for individuals . . . for families . . . yes, for nations. Why does the Holy Spirit want intercession for nations and their leaders? There is an alien afoot, an interloper who encroaches as much as possible in any life, any home, any business, any land—to crowd in by whatever bold or subtle tactic and to diminish God's inheritance for that person or people.

The serpent slowly winds his coils around hearts, and crushes them;

around homes, and crumbles them;

around leaders, and breaks them;

around enterprises, and smashes them;

around bodies, and destroys them;

around lands, and brings reproach upon them.

But something is happening—something good.

The people of the Lord are learning that Holy-Spirit-begotten righteousness is more than mere religiousness. It is being demonstrated in a willingness to pray as God leads. Like those believers who trusted God through the chance of the lot, there are more and more ready souls who will trust the chance promptings that come to their minds—thoughts of people or things which they interpret as the Holy Spirit's direction for prayer.

Many things which encroach upon life, which intrude upon

God-intended-joy for individuals, are calculated attacks of the adversary. He may invade God's boundaries, but a retaliatory force can drive him back. Intercessions can (1) recognize the appointment of God that we pray with power; (2) fall upon our king's enemies, knowing we have His authority to resist Satan with bold prayings in the Spirit, and (3) press. Yes, intercessions can press.

Intercessions press the border lines back to proper dimensions. Prayer sees that those lines reach unto the dimensions of God's destiny for a situation. The Father, who has ordained as we grow into the inheritance of an enlarged place of living and experience, taught David about this experience:

> He delivered me from my strong enemy, and from them which hated me: for they were too strong for me. They prevented me in the day of my calamity: but the LORD was my stay. He brought me forth also into a large place . . .(Psalm 18:17-19).

The keynote of this truth, however, is the recognition of our responsibility to wage a warfare that will not allow encroachment without counterattack. Intercession is far more than a mere synonym for prayer, it is an antonym for encroachment—an insistence that God's boundaries be observed and His landmarks observed.

18.
THE PRAYING THAT CONTRACTS WITH GOD

Supplication has been used interchangeably with prayer—earnest prayer, diligent prayer, fervent prayer—for so long that even some good translators have used the words as though they were identical. But the word must be preserved separately in our vocabulary, because it is possibly the most advanced aspect of the privilege of prayer.

Supplication cuts through the rag-tag affairs of earth and man at their most decadent and lays hold of God's sovereign order. That's why we call it "praying that contracts with God." The eternal God has an established order for all things—an order which was determined before the world began and has been decreed according to His eternal will. Supplication reaches to call forth from the Almighty the reinstatement of His original decree in whatever matters we bring before Him. Since God does have an intended purpose regarding any specific matter, we are contracting with Him for the executing of that issue in perfect line and timing with His eternal counsels and decrees. This is in accordance with the authority which He has granted us, the church, through His Son Jesus.

Supplication may at first seem to be no more than "praying in the will of God," or "asking according to His will," or 'interceding to the intent that what boundaries He intended from the beginning be reestablished." But there is an essential difference. It is time. Supplication is (1) a continual praying—an ongoing quest for a given matter to be settled in God's will and, (2) it is also a contingent praying—a quest for God's order in God's timing.

Both involve time: the first, by the passage of time during continued prayer. This is not so much to focus on the duration of any one given season of prayer, but to emphasize the consistent bearing up of a matter in prayer over a period of time—as long as it takes.

The second concerns the contingency of God's timing. What creates this contingency is not God's will and power, but man's. There are innumerable matters brought before the Father in prayer which are inextricably bound up in other lives and circumstances than the one immediately being prayed for. An answer for one person requires His dealing in others as well, for He honors the limitations imposed on the circumstances by disobedient men. What they have willed He will not contradict, but the glory of His wisdom is His ability to supercede man's doings. His foolishness is still wiser than man's wisdom. Virtually no request involves any long-term difficulty or number of people but that an answer of any kind carries in it a kind of domino principle. Touch one and many are affected.

Nothing happens for the blessing of mankind without a struggle. To understand that, we need to look at the cross where Jesus died. Not even God could redeem man or solve the infinitely complex puzzle of how the tangle of lives in sin might be unraveled without His own suffering and death.

It took time. It took God entering the context of time.

And it took supplication.

Hebrews 5:1-9, in relating the ministry of our Lord Jesus Christ as the high priest of our salvation, reminds us of "the days of his flesh," with specific emphasis upon the nature and fact of His supplication (v. 7). The word is significant to our understanding, for in Gethsemane when Jesus was pleading as a human being—anticipating the agony of Calvary and the separation from life—He pled: "If it be possible let this cup pass from me."

He was asking if there were anything in the eternal order of things that would allow for an adjusted pathway of delivering mankind from destruction. But His perfect humanity continues, "Nevertheless not my will, but thine, be done" (Luke 22:42). He settles on what He knows to be the divine order: Without the shedding of blood—no remission of sins. In the executive council chambers of eternity—before the world was—the lamb agreed to this moment (I Peter 1:19, 20; Hebrews 9:24-28; Revelation 13:8). Then He lived it out in the context of time. What was willed from before the world was born in the travail of tears and agony of blood, which, according to Hebrews 5, was supplication.

This is awesome in its implications, for the theological ramifications stagger the mind, boggle the best intellects, and tend to promote debate rather than plain praying. And it is awesome in its cost. Hence, the inclination to debate. It's preferable to talk than to die; to nitpick creedal straws than to lay on the altar of prayer and be consumed with the passion of supplication.

Supplication is best understood from this beginning point: the cross of Christ. Seeing Jesus approach it is the best illustration of supplication, and it is from the blood He shed there that all authority for supplication is secured on our part. There is nothing for which I shall supplicate—nothing for which I shall plead the establishing of God's eternally intended order—but that the right to ask is granted and the power to answer is released through His cross.

No grander concept in prayer exists than this right to enter into praying which is bent on seeing His eternal counsels manifest among mankind. Through the blood of the everlasting covenant, you and I may determine the fulfillment of His will on earth.

He has decreed salvation.

His side of the contract is signed—in His own blood.

Now He waits.

He is waiting for those who will give themselves to the kind of praying that is providing the verbal countersignature which releases His decreed will upon those for whom we supplicate. The contract is effectual when both signatures are fixed. Neither works independently. The partnership is the key to the release. That's the contract.

Near Caesarea-Philippi, on the lower slopes of Mount Hermon, Jesus first announced His intent to establish the church. Peter had answered His inquiry—"Who do you say that I am?"—by declaring, "Thou art the Christ, the Son of the living God" (Matthew 16:16). After commending Peter, and answering with joy, Jesus said: "I will build my church, and the gates of hell shall not prevail against it." Two facts are disclosed here:

1. Christ Jesus states His plan to develop a spiritual force comprised of a group of people. He is not speaking of an institution but a "church" which is a group of people who have exited the present order of things—in which most people are gripped. Like an army, this church is made up of people who are being shaped and shod with character and power, to introduce a new order among mankind in which peace and purpose are newly possible.

2. In speaking of the "gates of hell," He has not described

His church's mission as one preoccupied with economic reforms, militaristic advance, or political power. Hell's "gates" bespeak the counsels of darkness—the plots, ploys and plunderings of satanic origin which are spawned in the spirit realm and erupt in the physical. He says, "Hell shall be assaulted and shall not withstand my troops."

Then Jesus said, "I will give unto you the keys of the kingdom of heaven, and whatever you bind on earth will be bound in heaven and whatever you loose on earth will be loosed in heaven." The keys indicate "right" or "authority." The possession of a key is the signal that one "has a right" to enter a given domain. In this case, Jesus says, "I am giving you the right to function in the domain of the Almighty. I am authorizing you to transact certain functions in the spiritual realm, all the while opposing hell's counsels as you do."

The words "bind" (*deo*) and "supplicate" (*deesis*) are near to one another in the Greek dictionary. Their relationship, however, is more than alphabetical proximity. Concepts fit together when the biblical practice of praying with supplications is unfolded in the light of its use in the early church.

When Christ said, "Whatever you bind on earth," He employed a term that contains more than the mere meaning of "tying"—although it does include that sense as well. But since He said, "shall be bound in heaven," we know we're dealing with a spiritual principle, not an earthly cord.

We also use the word "bind" in contractual relations: "I'm bound by my word"; "The terms of the contract are binding." Such use notes factors more powerful than hemp, chain or cable. Those factors are words—spoken words.

"For ever, O LORD, thy word is settled in heaven" (Psalm 119:89).

God deals in words.

When He speaks, He creates. When He decrees, it is established. When He promises, it is a certainty awaiting fulfillment. His Word is foundational; you can build on it. "He that hears my words and does them is like a man who builds on a rock," Jesus said.

And His words are powerful too. You can bind with them.

The essence of supplication is this:

1. I accept the premise that God has decreed that certain matters are to be.

2. Whenever I encounter circumstances or situations in which His benevolent or righteous decrees are obviously not ruling, I pray.

3. My prayer is a calling forth of what He has willed but which cannot be released on earth until someone here calls for it.

4. My prayer is prevailing prayer that continues relentlessly, all the while believing that the waiting is not worthless, but is that period in which God clears up other matters to make way for the release of the matter concerning which I prayed.

The word for supplication, *deesis*, occurs nineteen times in the New Testament. In all cases at least one of three things is in evidence in the prayer described: (a) a plea for the *usual*, the created order of life to take place, whereas it has apparently been hindered until now. Example: Zacharias' prayer that his barren wife be blessed with a child ("your *deesis* is heard" Luke 1:13); (b) a stedfast continuity in regular and unceasing prayers, indicating a tireless pursuit of a given goal. Example: The prayers of the Philippian church for Paul's release from prison in Rome ("this shall turn to my rescue through your *deesis*" Philippians 1:19); or, (c) an intense spiritual struggle is being engaged in, in which the issue will determine with far-reaching effect the whole work of the kingdom of God. Example: In the great passage on the spiritual conflict, Ephesians, chapter 6, the command to supplication caps off the whole instruction on being properly armed ("praying always with all prayer and *deesis* . . ." v. 18).

Supplications are pleas for God's ordained order to appear. Supplications prevail above earth-powers. Supplications overthrow hell-powers.

When Jesus announced, "Whatever you bind on earth shall be bound in heaven, and whatever you loose on earth shall be loosed in heaven," what He meant can only be fully appreciated by our bothering with a simple lesson in Greek verb forms. Here's what He said:

"Whatever you bind" (*deses*)—Matthew 16:19—here the verb is aorist in tense, subjunctive in mood and active in voice. That may be just so much tedious information for most readers, but the force of His invitation to us is so great that we need to exercise all the precision we can to insure our grasping it as well as possible.

To explain, the form has this effect on the verb *deo*, to bind:

1. The tense (aorist) features *a given point in time*.
2. The mood (subjunctive) features *contingency*, the *conditional*—you might, and then again, you might not.
3. The voice (active) features a conscious, *responsible participation*.

Before we put it all together, we need to note exactly what He said following that. He said, "Whatever you bind . . . shall be bound" (*estai dedemenon*). Again we parse the words employed:

1. *estai*, future tense of to be, meaning *"it shall be."*
2. *dedemenon*, perfect, passive participle of *deo*:
   a. The tense (perfect) features a completed act;

139

b. The voice (passive) features the fact that we are recipients of action that was performed by another; and

c. The participial form is like an adverb, qualifying the earlier form of the verb "to be."

Now, what does all this say?

Here is a careful amplification of Jesus' words when He said I'll give you the keys to the kingdom:

> Whatever you may at any time encounter (of hell's counsels which I'm declaring my church shall prevail against), you will then face a decision as to whether you will or won't bind it. What transpires will be conditional upon your response. If you do personally and consciously involve yourself in the act of binding the issue on earth, you will discover that at that future moment when you do, that it has already been bound in heaven!

Astounding!

In short we are told by our Lord, "Whenever you determine to lay claim to the Father's counsels as opposed to the adversary's, you'll find that earth can have what heaven has already d\>cided on!"

The whole excursion into Greek grammar is essential, because phenomenal numbers of sincere, even devoted, teachers of the Word of God would prefer to avoid the potential impact of these words. And to a degree, it is understandable that they might. Despite the fact that those words call us to an uncanny responsibility in partnership with our God, a lot of folderol has gone on under the guise of "binding and loosing." Energetic antics, enthusiastic babble and fanatical claims—which, as a rule, are eventually followed by disappointment and confusion—have smogged the air around this vital portion of what Christ taught.

But here are pointers to help establish the wise use of these words, as well as to enlighten us as to their meaning:

140

1. Binding is not some whirlwind rush into the spirit-realm like a posse chasing some demon behind a cactus and then lassoing it. Binding is contracting with God. I am saying: "Father, what *you* have willed, I call forth upon earth!"

2. Whatever boldness we may exercise in binding is only because grounds for our action have already been established: the cross—the blood of Jesus. That's what makes possible any actuating of the contract now. The authority is not in our knowledge, in our boldness, in our demeanor or in our tone of voice. It's in Him—Christ the Lord. He died, and drained off hell's powers by swallowing them up in himself. Remembering this keeps our privilege of authority in pure balance. This perspective will maintain a proper boldness with humility.

3. And it is contingent upon timing. Some things won't happen in the visible realm immediately. That is not to say that if nothing happens, pretend like it really is happening invisibly and don't feel too badly if it never surfaces where you can see it. No. This is to say, rather, that continual prayer will be appropriate—yes, required—in many cases. Large issues have long-range consequences that may require a lot of time to work out.

The same verb construction is employed in the words "Whatever you loose on earth shall be loosed in heaven." The order in which the two verb sets occur indicates that in "binding" we are calling forth God's eternal counsels—His changeless will—with reference to a subject, a person, a need, a circumstance. Then, once His will comes into operation, the glory of His grace begins His work—release! "After you call for the contracted plan," Jesus seems to say, "we can get about the matter of setting people free!"

And isn't this God's plan, after all?

Didn't He intend that?

According to the creator's intent, man ought to be free. Free from sin, free from self-centeredness, free from sickness, free from barrenness, free from bondage, free from compulsion to do evil . . . free.

Free willed.

Free to choose his master, and free to worship his creator.

This is the freedom that ought to be, but so often isn't.

And supplications make the difference.

The Greek particle for "ought" is *dei*. It argues for moral, legal, rational integrity—"it ought to be." An etymological connection may exist between this word and *deesis*.

Deo, "to bind,"

Dei, "ought,"

Deesis, "supplication."

They run in a string. And they are irretrievably tied together as the Word unfolds the truth, line upon line and precept upon precept.

Supplication (*deesis*) is that intense, prevailing prayer form that binds (*deo*) over to earth what ought (*dei*) to be experienced here, according to God's eternal counsels.

God has contracted for man's redemption and blessing, and signed for it in blood. Supplication is the work of those who won't stop until they see that contract fulfilled.

God doesn't need to be convinced.

But hell's gates must be.

They will prevail until we do.

It's up to me

. . . and you, too.

19.
A WORD IN CONCLUSION,
about the dangers of development, and the beauty of balance.

Teaching about prayer contains, ironically, a hidden danger. We can think that because we have learned something about it, we therefore know how to do it. But that is as foolish as supposing that a person has become an upholsterer simply because he took a course in upholstering. People participate in athletic activities who are not athletes. So, understanding the principles of a subject, knowing the rules of a game, or reading a handbook about some craft does not perfect a person in a trade or a sport.

There is no substitute for doing the thing.

An elegantly completed chair, covered with a tastefully designed fabric and flawless in the craftsmanship which performed the work, is not a fluke. Neither is eighteen holes of golf with a score in the high sixties.

Each of these examples is the fruit of practice. Steady performance and efficiently expended effort result from the application of the principles on a regular basis.

The same is true of prayer. Practice perfects, matures, and

143

develops.

And this isn't double-talk.

Whatever has been said in earlier portions of this book to excite expectancy and urge the belief that God is a giving God, we are not now backtracking or hinting that such encouragement was all a confidence game—a happy "come-on."

God is no con man. And the promises and concepts with which we have dealt are His.

But with the understanding of prayer comes responsibility as well. Capturing the richness of the Bible's revelation about any particular theme is fulfilling, to say the least. But growing in the disciplines which that particular truth requires is a demanding proposition. And probably no truth is so demanding as prayer.

None of us learns those disciplines quietly.

Horatius Bonar, the great and godly preacher of a century past, known for his fidelity to the ways of the Lord and his walk before God in true discipleship, said, in the fifty-eighth year of his life, "I have never come to a time of prayer but that it has been with a struggle."

His honesty is encouraging.

With candor he declares what all of us learn to be so: "The spirit indeed is willing, but the flesh is weak. . . . To will is present with me; but how to perform that which is good I find not."

We're quick with the gun, but slow on the trigger.

Acknowledging this difficulty, the way in which the flesh *acts* upon the truth it learns is important for two reasons:

(1) Our intent has been to remove fogs and shadows that have generally made the privilege and practice of prayer

144

unclear or mysterious to many, so that we might move together in bold belief. Our study is not complete with the conclusion of the book. It merely begins with it.

(2) And since prayer holds such potential for releasing the power of God toward our world, we also need to establish a certain climate of caution.

This caution is not a hint that there is something to fear. Not at all. There are no hidden dynamite caps in the throne room of heaven, where each might be accidentally exploded by one of God's children to his hurt.

But the caution is against discouragement and presumption. Otherwise we might be tempted to abandon our aggressive posture and retreat to earlier stances of passivity in prayer.

Brace against discouragement, because there is a great temptation to suppose that once a prayer-key is found, it should fit anything, any time.

Expect this temptation.

It isn't sowing doubt to forecast its rise. It will come. Discouragement will raise its head because it's tempting for me to suppose that because I have learned something of the Father's way that I just might understand all His ways. But something learned isn't everything and growth in His ways will be acquired as I continue with prayer.

The Bible discloses that "All the paths of the LORD are mercy and truth . . ." (Psalm 25:10), but also asserts, "How unsearchable are his judgments and his ways past finding out!" (Romans 11:33). Of Moses, it is said that the Lord showed him His ways (Psalm 103:7), but you can count on it that He didn't show him all of them! There is a continual state of dependence that is appropriate even in the most learned saint. David exemplifies it in the words, "Show me thy ways, O LORD; teach me thy paths. Lead me in thy truth, and teach me: for thou art

145

the God of my salvation; on thee do I wait all the day" (Psalm 25:4, 5).

To avoid the discouragement that might come when we fail to "get anything to happen" by prayer, we should seek to grow in His ways. I may not yet have mastered anything, but it doesn't mean I'm not going anywhere! I am committed to continue

. . . learning to understand His heart,
. . . trusting in the certainty of His Word.
. . . waiting with patience for His time and
. . . listening quietly for His voice.

These commitments will neutralize discouragement's power. And they will carry me toward the kind of maturity that is not only undaunted by temporary trials, but which sees each barricade to victory smashed beneath the power of God.

Then, the matter of *presumption*.

Presumption lies not in believing for too much, but thinking you are believingly invading an issue, when you are only carnally barging your way in. It is a persistent trait that we must continually guard against. The "bull in the china shop" syndrome has been demonstrated by many who "claimed authority" but didn't really function in faith.

And we are *sheep* not bulls; children, not bulldozers.

Presumption is rooted in fear and fostered in pride. It begins when I am afraid that God won't swing into action fast enough if I don't do something colorful to prove my faith. And it flourishes when I foolishly make high-sounding noises about "faith" and "trusting God." Human pride always has to prove itself. But not so with the praying servant of God. The signs *follow*. It's wise to wait for them rather than try to make them happen.

Nothing can make us invulnerable to presumption. Satan invited Jesus to demonstrate His faith by leaping from the

146

towering wall by the Temple in Jerusalem. It is the sort of thing he still urges upon people who pray and fast as their Master did.

But presumption can be as certainly avoided as discouragement.

The precautionary keys are *humility* and *patience*.

Humility is one of the most abused words in the language, particularly among spiritually minded people, who display everything from the genuine article to unreasonable facsimiles. Sadly, the mild, the bland and the innocuous are often called "humble"—generally because they don't possess enough strength of character to gain a more positive distinction.

But true humility, by definition of the Greek word *prautes*, is *strong*. *Praus* (the adjective) described a mighty stallion that had been trained for battle, broken but retaining the dynamic of its inherent nature (see Kittel's *Theological Dictionary*, VI, 645). The difference between this wonderful creature and his wild counterpart is that its dynamic had been brought under the control of his master. A touch of the rein, and a ton of horseflesh was *directed*. Nothing of its spirit broken, only its self-will.

Thus humility, in reference to boldness in prayer, is *not* some rationalized surrender to circumstance: "We prayed, and nothing happened. I guess we must bow humbly to the will of God." That's a passivity that is as willful and presumptuous as impulsive grandstanding.

Peter and John were bold to take the crippled man's hand (Acts 3:1-11) and command him to stand as a demonstration of the fact that Jesus Christ the Lord had healed him instantaneously! Their boldness was exhibited in humility—without presumption.

See what controls the power: "And as Peter and John went up together into the temple at the hour of prayer . . ." (v. 1).

147

There it is.

They were en route to prayer.

Two praying men, on their way to pray some more. This is the key to knowing God's time for boldness: *prayer.*

Wise counsel is in Peter's words written at a later date: "Humble yourselves therefore under the mighty hand of God, that he may exalt you in due time: casting all your care upon him; for he careth for you" (I Peter 5:6, 7).

Triumph is the inevitable experience of the humble.

But not of the mild . . .

    nor of the will-o'-the-wisp . . .

        nor of the erstwhile pray-er.

But triumph is available to the unpresumptuous.

And with that, an added word about patience —unhurriedness. We need to learn the warnings of wisdom:

"He that is hasty of spirit exalts foolishness" (Proverbs 14:29).

"He that hasteth with his feet sinneth" (Proverbs 19:2).

"Go not forth hastily to strive, lest thou know not what to do in the end thereof, when thy neighbour hath put thee to shame" (Proverbs 25:8).

"Seest thou a man that is hasty in his words? There is more hope of a fool than of him" (Proverbs 29:20).

The counsel of Scripture urges considered action in all things. The situation may be desperate, but God isn't. Time is never our enemy when we are dealing with the eternal one. True prayer is always mindful that the acid test isn't split-second answers. But we should not doubt that such quick responses will come at times.

While a number of Scriptures evidence my right to ask God to "Make haste and help me" (Psalm 70:1, 5; 38:22; 71:12, 141:1), there are none that allow my reckless haste in action or words when torment or trial, difficulty or dilemma confront me. The constant summons to us who pray is to make our prayer known and then wait with worship and patience:

> Don't let anything stir you to anxiety. Rather, in everything that concerns you, let your requests be spoken to God through prayers and supplications. Then, add to that praying a constant flow of thanksgiving, for that climate of praise is one in which God's peace flourishes; and that peace shall protect your heart and mind from turmoil and confusion—all this, through the power of our Lord Jesus Christ (Philippians 4:6, 7, paraphrase).

There are desirable graces the Father seeks to develop in all of us, and patience has a way of nourishing them all toward maturity. "Let patience have her perfecting effect on your life" (James 1:4); "For you have need of patience, that after you have done God's will you may receive the promise He has spoken" (Hebrews 10:36). Taking paraphrastic liberties with Romans 5:3-5, we can enlarge on the point in the spirit of the Word.

> Ah yes, I glory in the trials and troubles that I face, for I know they develop patience. Then, patience—as I am borne up through the trial by the Holy Spirit's help—produces experience. By experience, I mean that accumulating record of occasions in which I have proven God faithful under test. Trials test me, I call on Him, and though at times it seems long, He never fails. That's what gives rise to endless hope—my genuine expectancy with confidence. For God's love, poured out in our hearts by the Holy Spirit, is the guarantee that we shall never be embarrassed by a failure on His part.

There is a beauty in balance.

However, there is a subtle pride in spiritual passivity that calls itself patience and isn't. It is surrender to the snake. It surrenders to his operations, and then has the nerve to call what it suffers, by reason of the absence of bold confrontation, patience . . . or humility.

How can I know the difference?

The way I learn everything else on this subject.

Doing it.

Praying.

We are well advised to study the subject; we are well instructed to beware of discouragement and presumption; we are well counseled toward balance.

But we are best directed to pray.